MAK

(

THE ART OF AUTHENTICITY

ENCHANTING EBBS JOURNAL

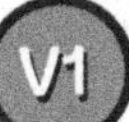

WITH FUN & UNIQUE ILLUSTRATIONS TO COLOR

MICHELLE GAUTHIER

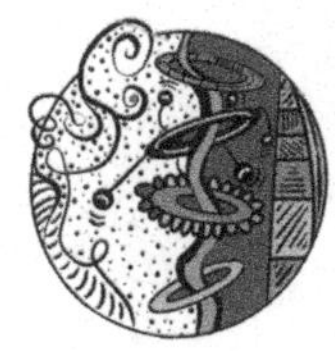

Make No Mistake Coloring
Fort Collins, Colorado

Illustrations: Michelle Gauthier
Cover Design: Liz Mrofka, BugleBox.com

ISBN-13: 979-8-9935250-0-6

To learn more about Make No Mistake Coloring and our products, visit MakeNoMistakeColoring.com

Connect with us at:
Facebook.com/MakeNoMistakeColoring
Instagram.com/MakeNoMistakeColoring

Acknowledgement & Dedication

I'd like to acknowledge Robin Shukle from What if? Ideation and Liz Mrofka from Bugle Box as this truly would not have happened but for them!

I'd like to dedicate this to my husband and son who believed in me and encouraged me every step of the way.

About this Journal

The fun, whimsical designs in this book are intended to allow freedom and relaxation before you begin your journaling adventure. The images are playful and open to the artist's interpretation. There is no right or wrong way to color these pages. Choose one color or the whole box of colors. Bring the images, and your thoughts, to life with your own authentic style.

While anyone can experience the joy of coloring, my designs are made for those seeking stress, depression and/or anxiety relief. For neurodivergent individuals such as those with autism and ADHD/ADD coloring can be particularly beneficial as the repetitive motions and focus involved in coloring can help improve concentration and reduce impulsivity.

Journaling offers several significant benefits for mental health by providing a safe, private space for self-expression and introspection. It is known to help with stress reduction, since writing about stressful events helps to regulate emotions and provides a cognitive break from worry, lowering overall anxiety levels. It can also offer a tangible way to sort through complex feelings like anger, sadness, or fear, helping you move from raw reaction to thoughtful response.

Whether you color, journal or both, I hope you enjoy it!

Where to Find My Reflections

Reflection	Page #

Where to Find My Reflections

Reflection	Page #

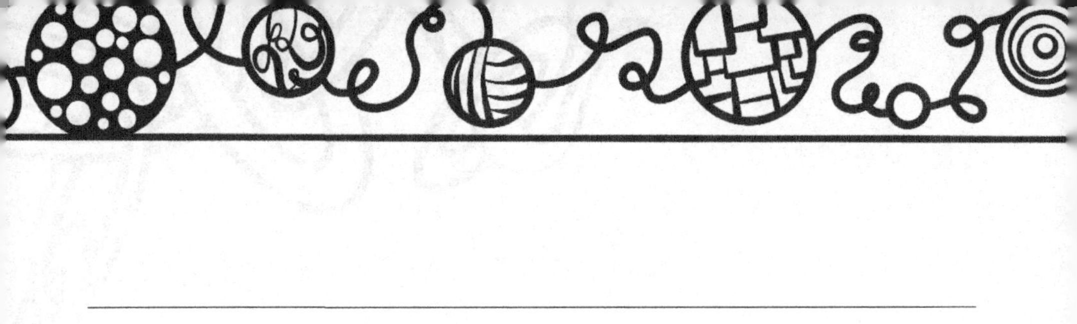

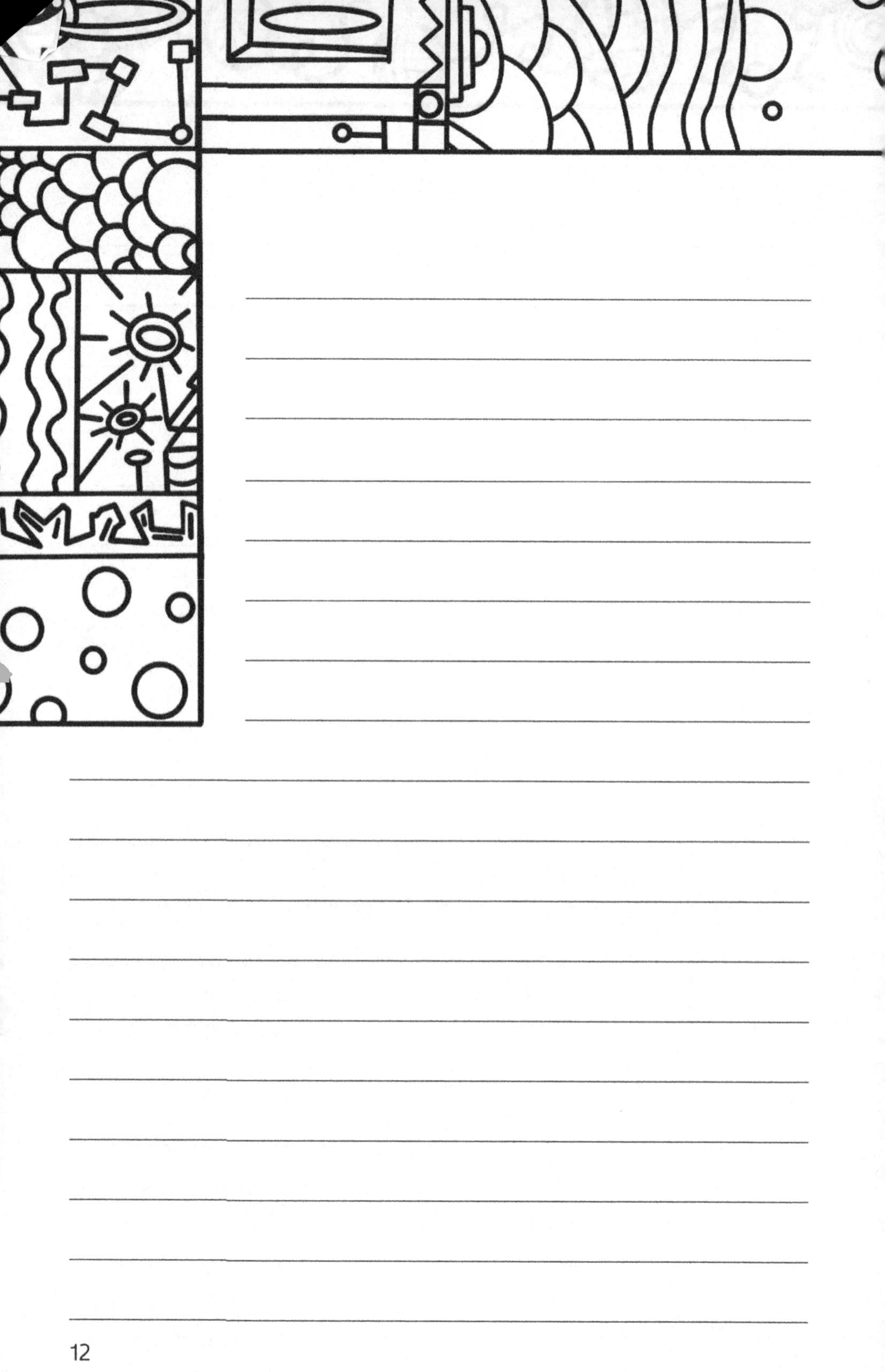

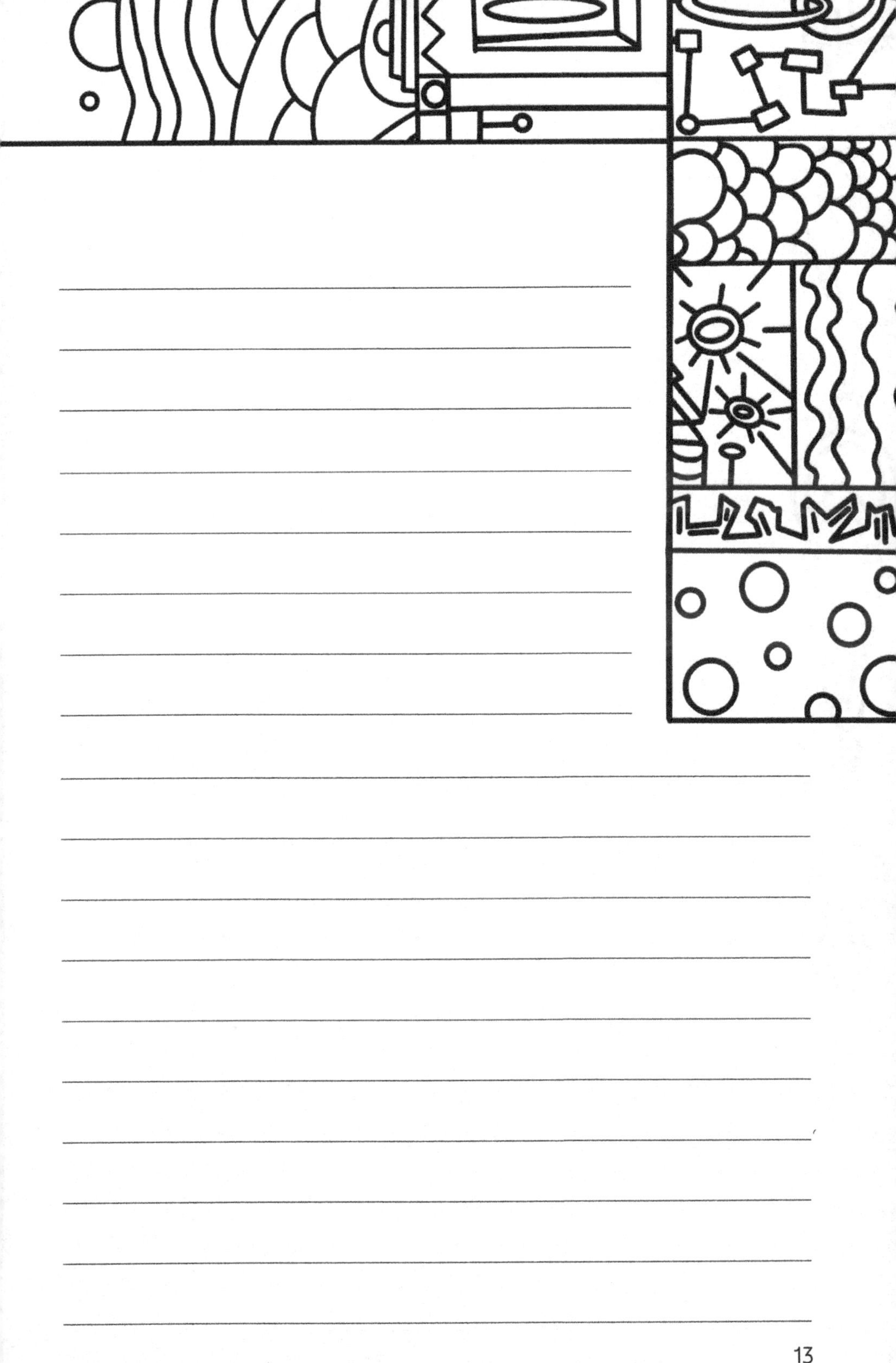

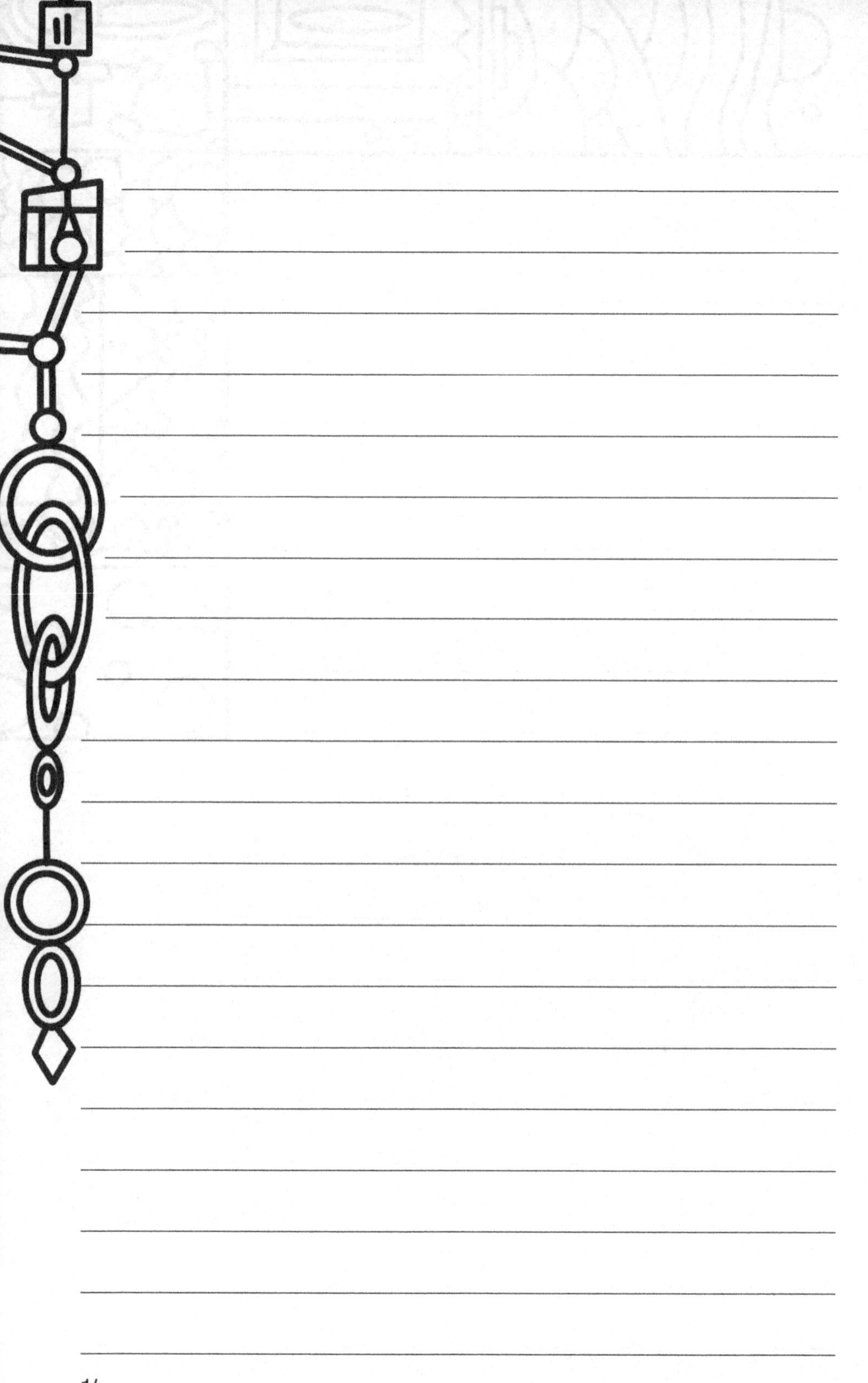

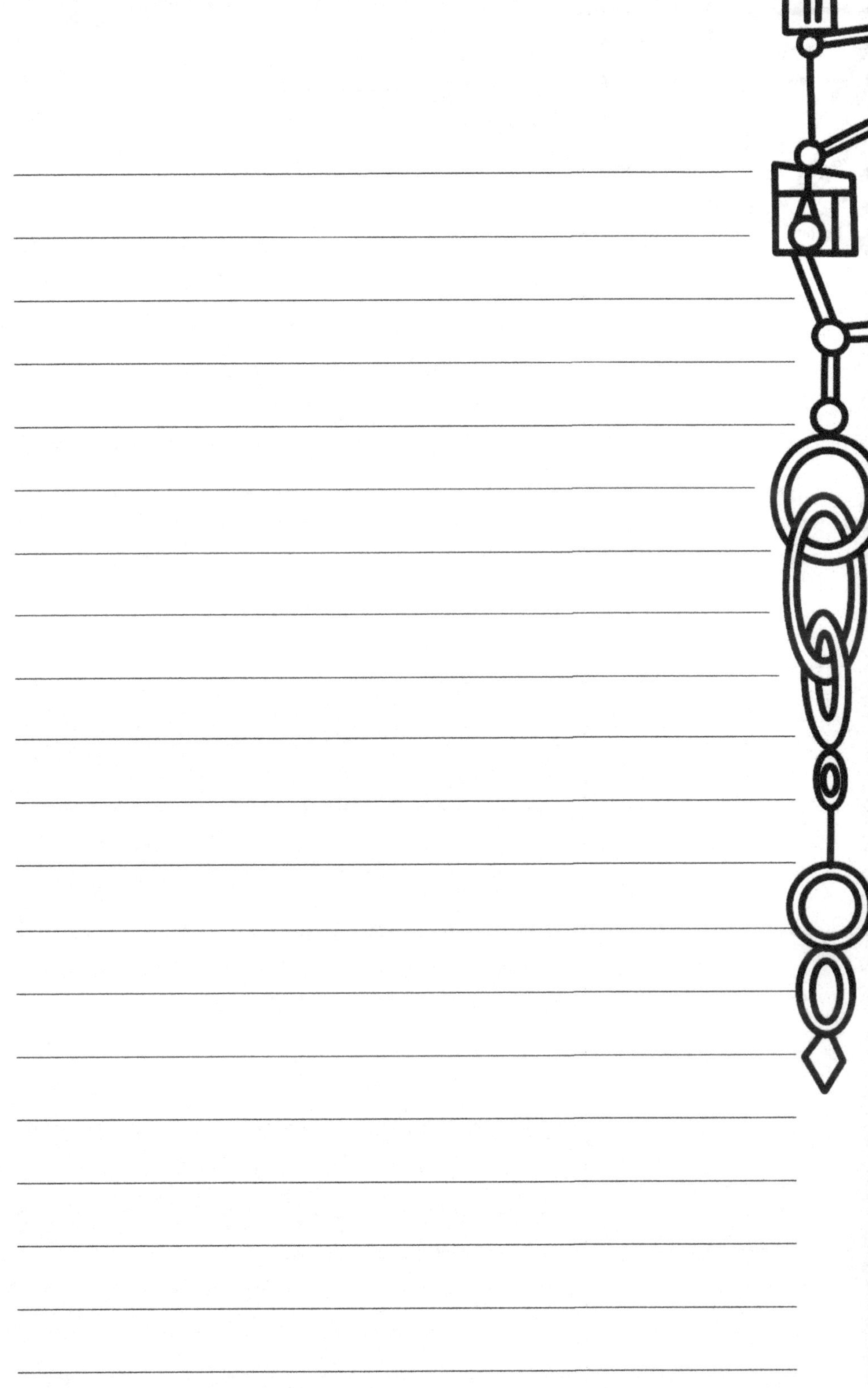

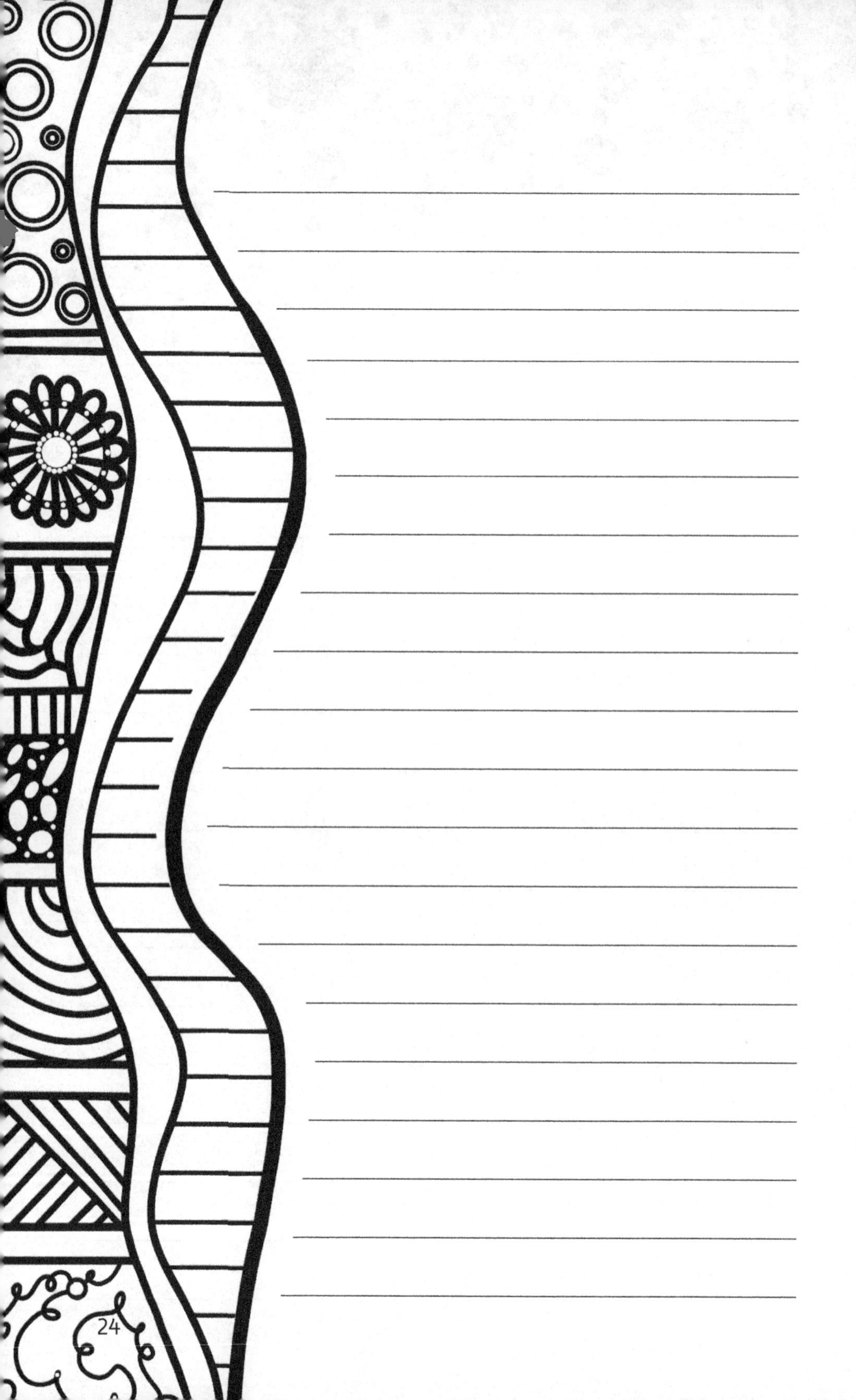

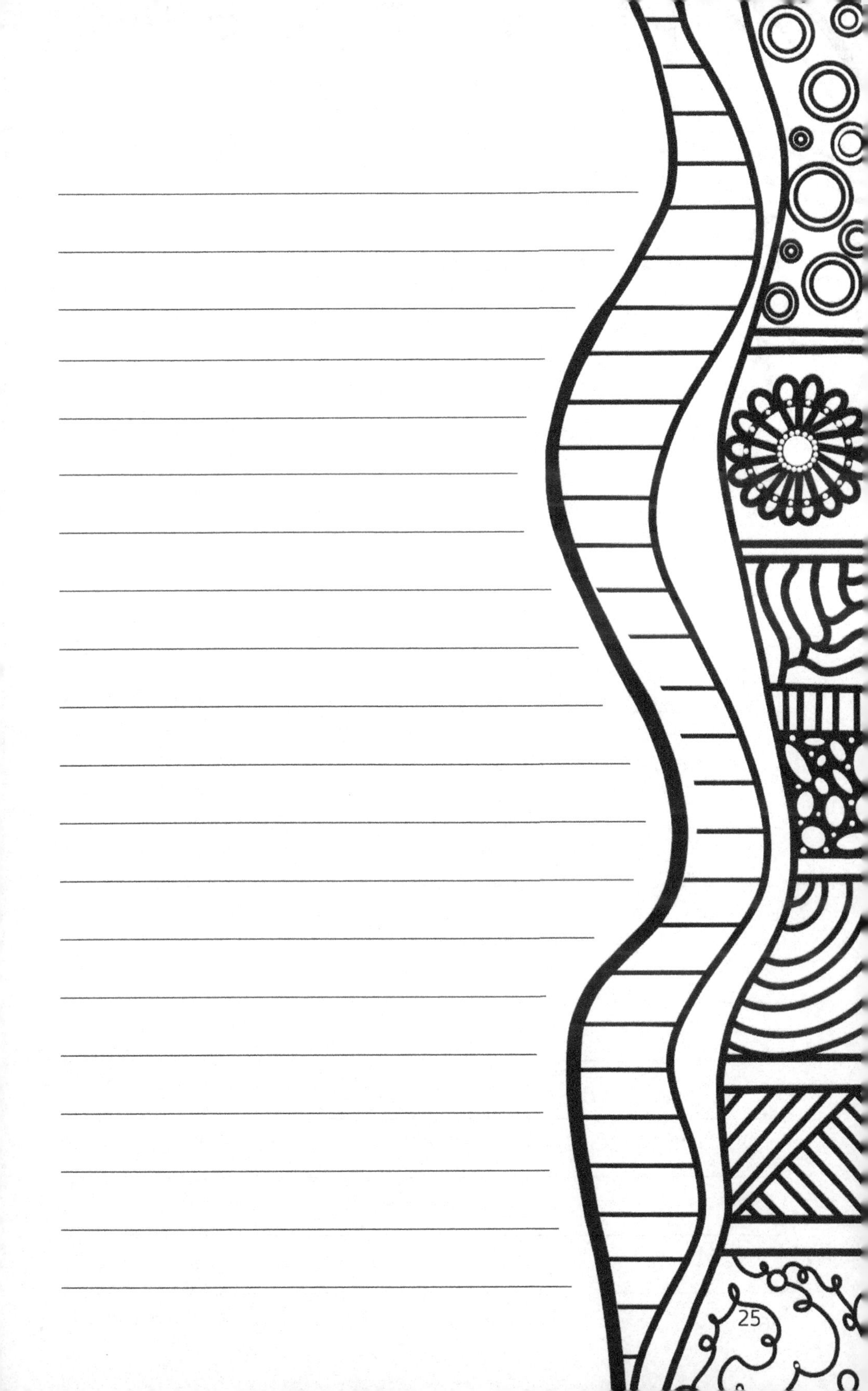

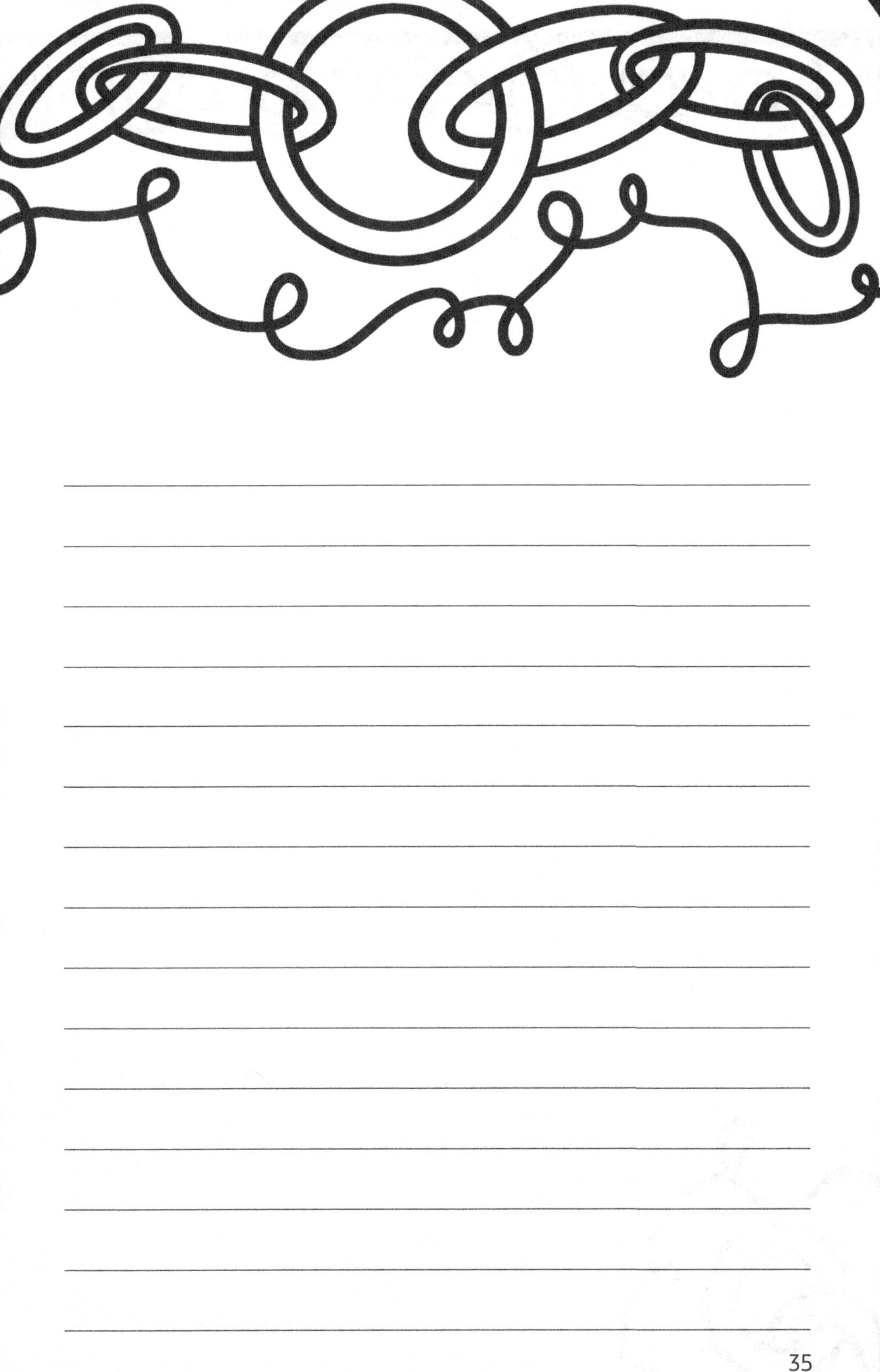

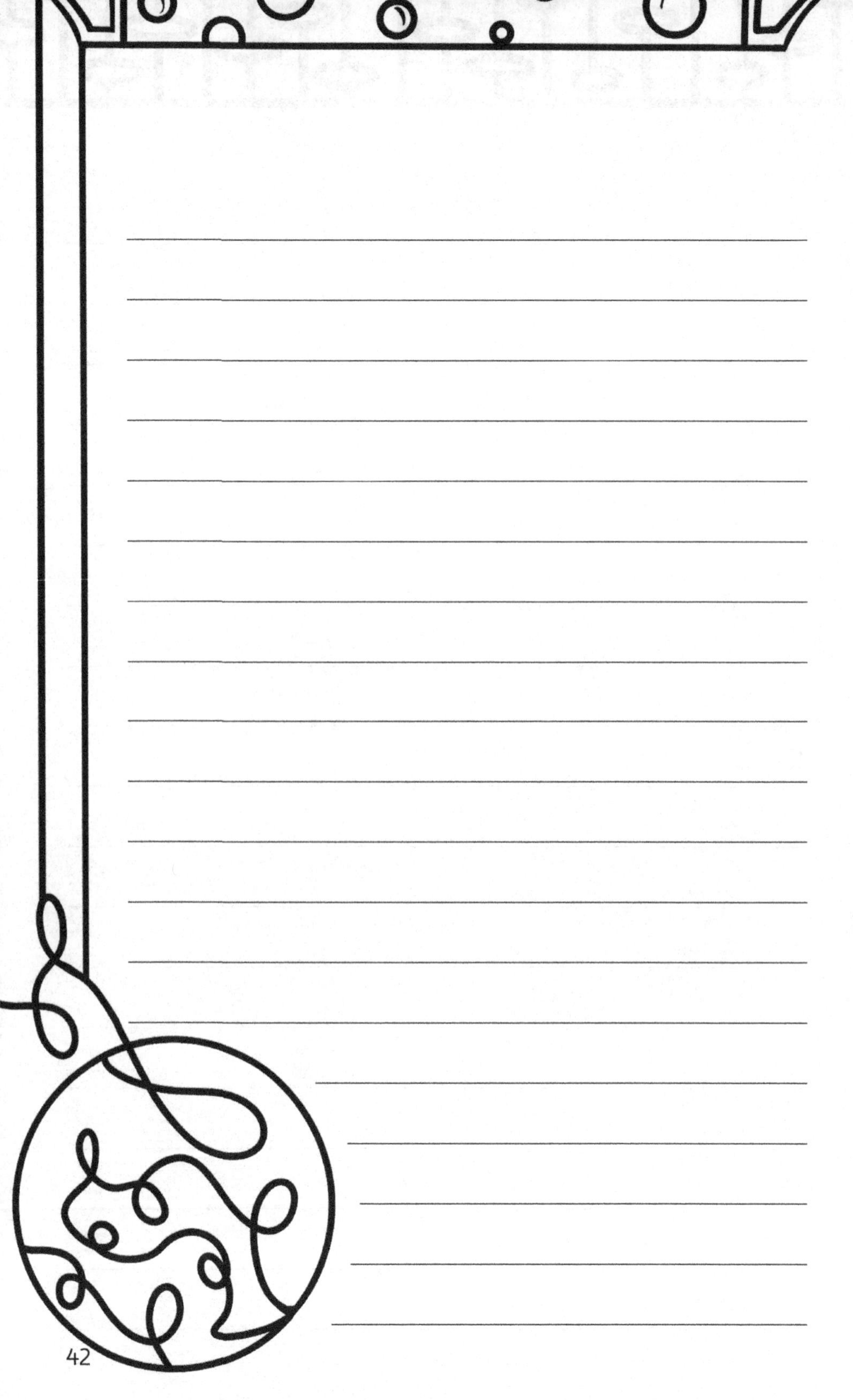

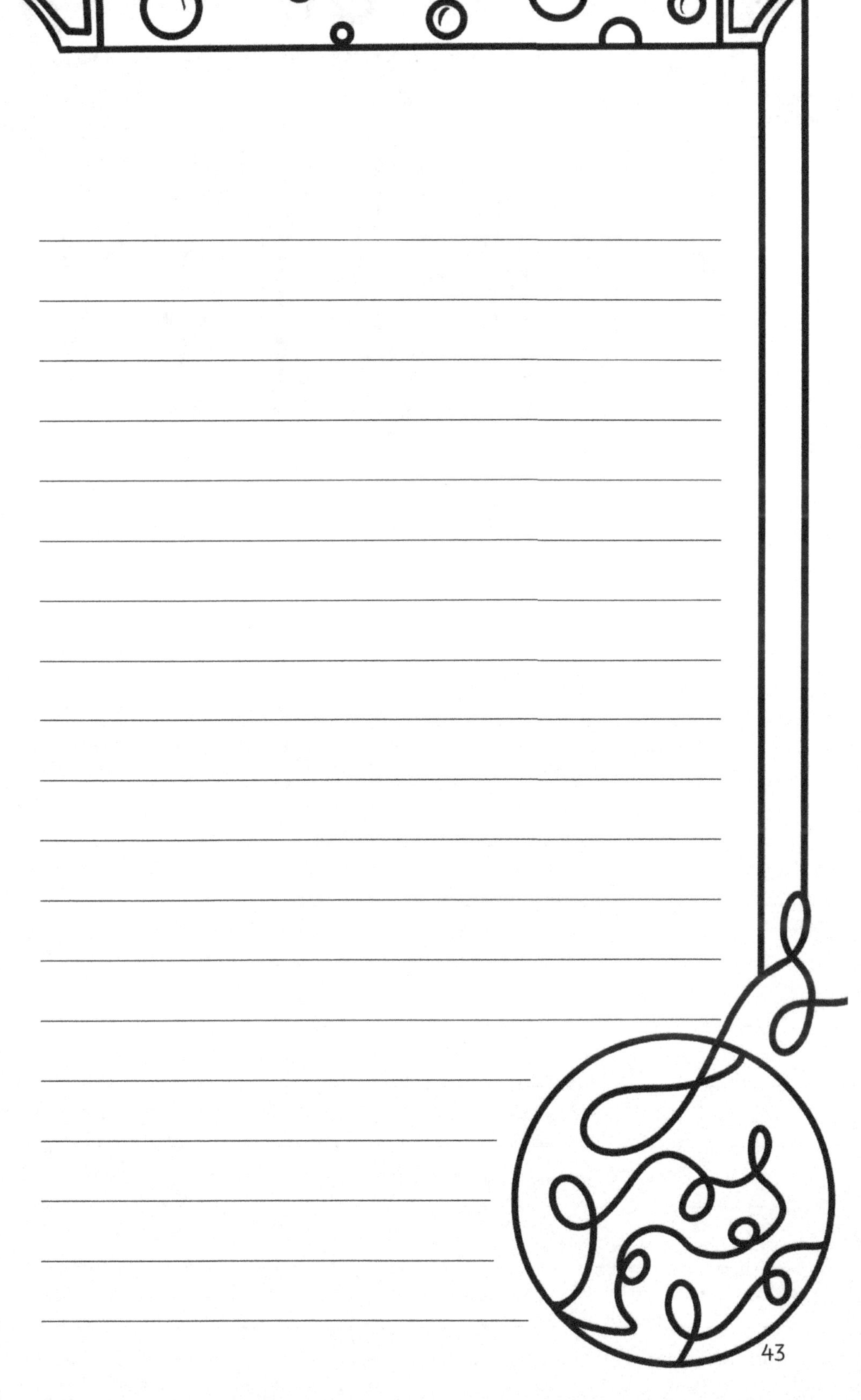

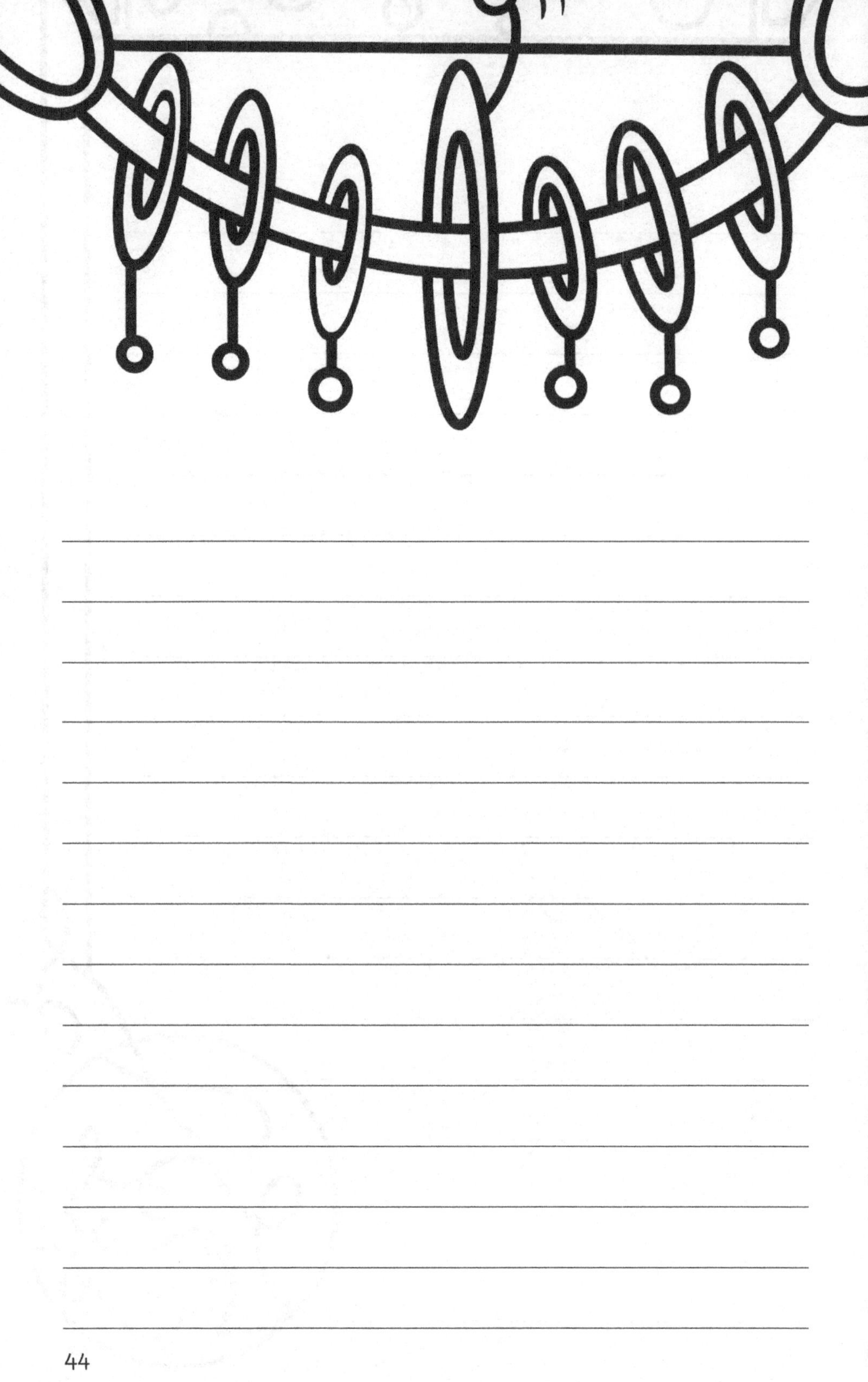

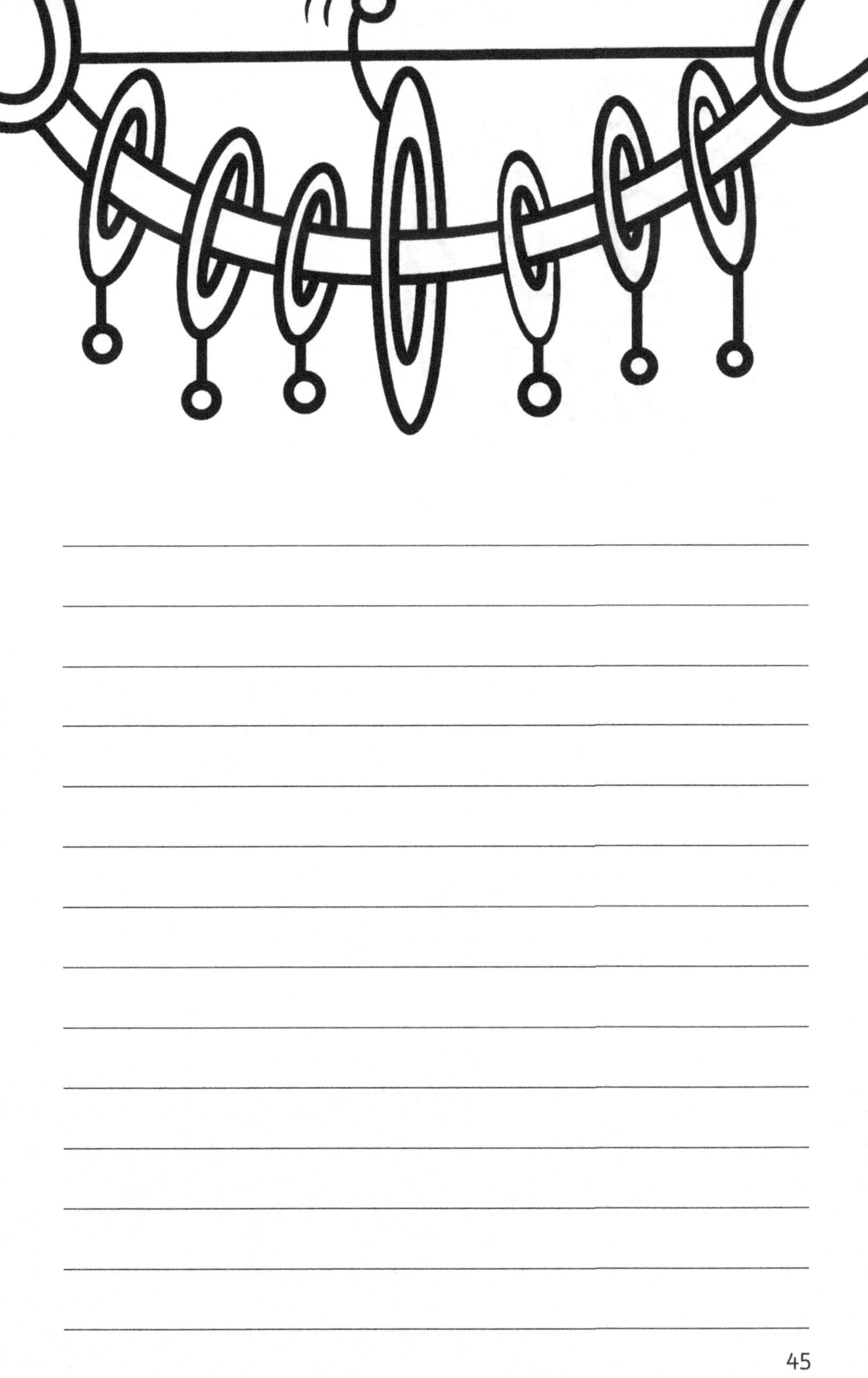

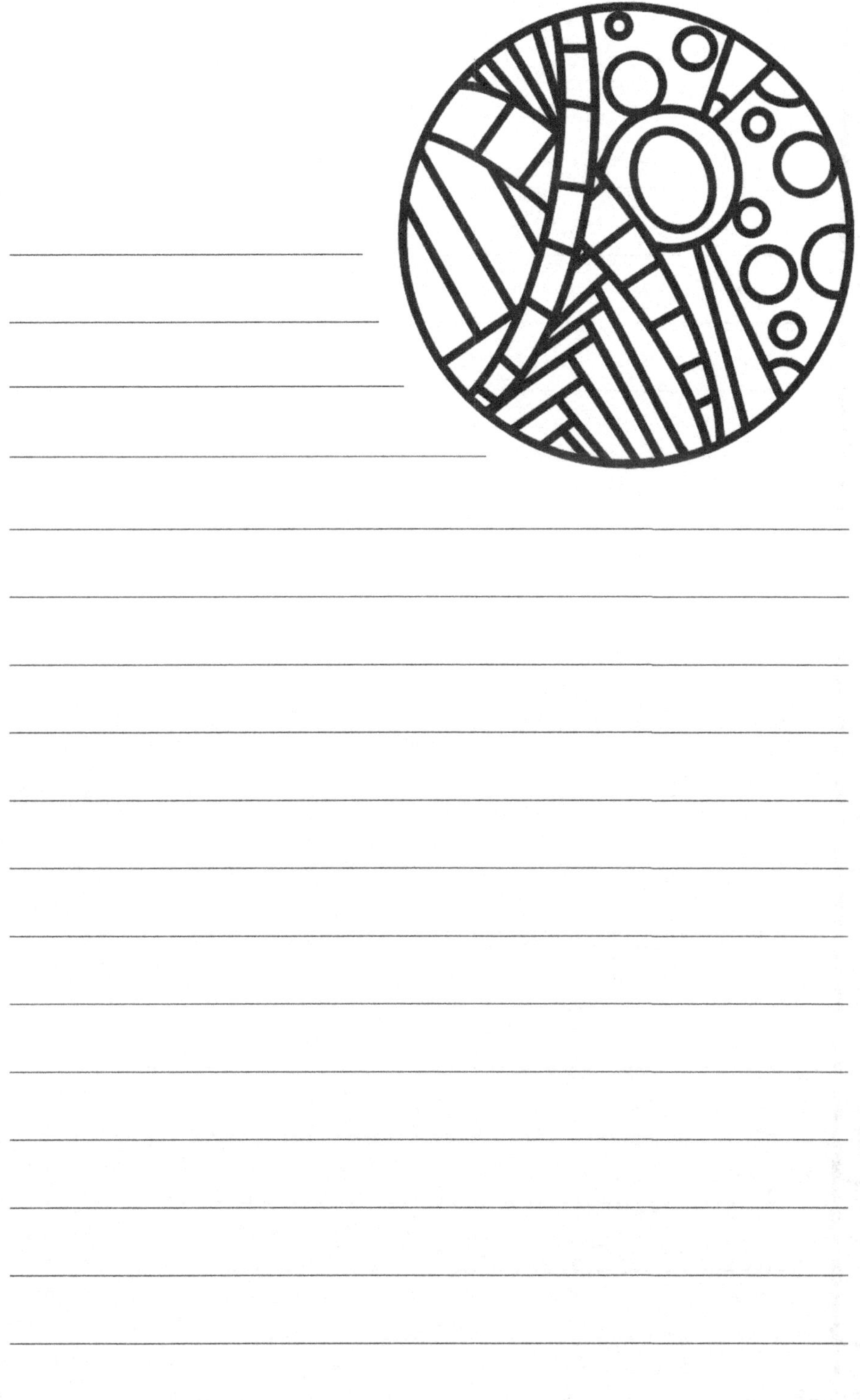

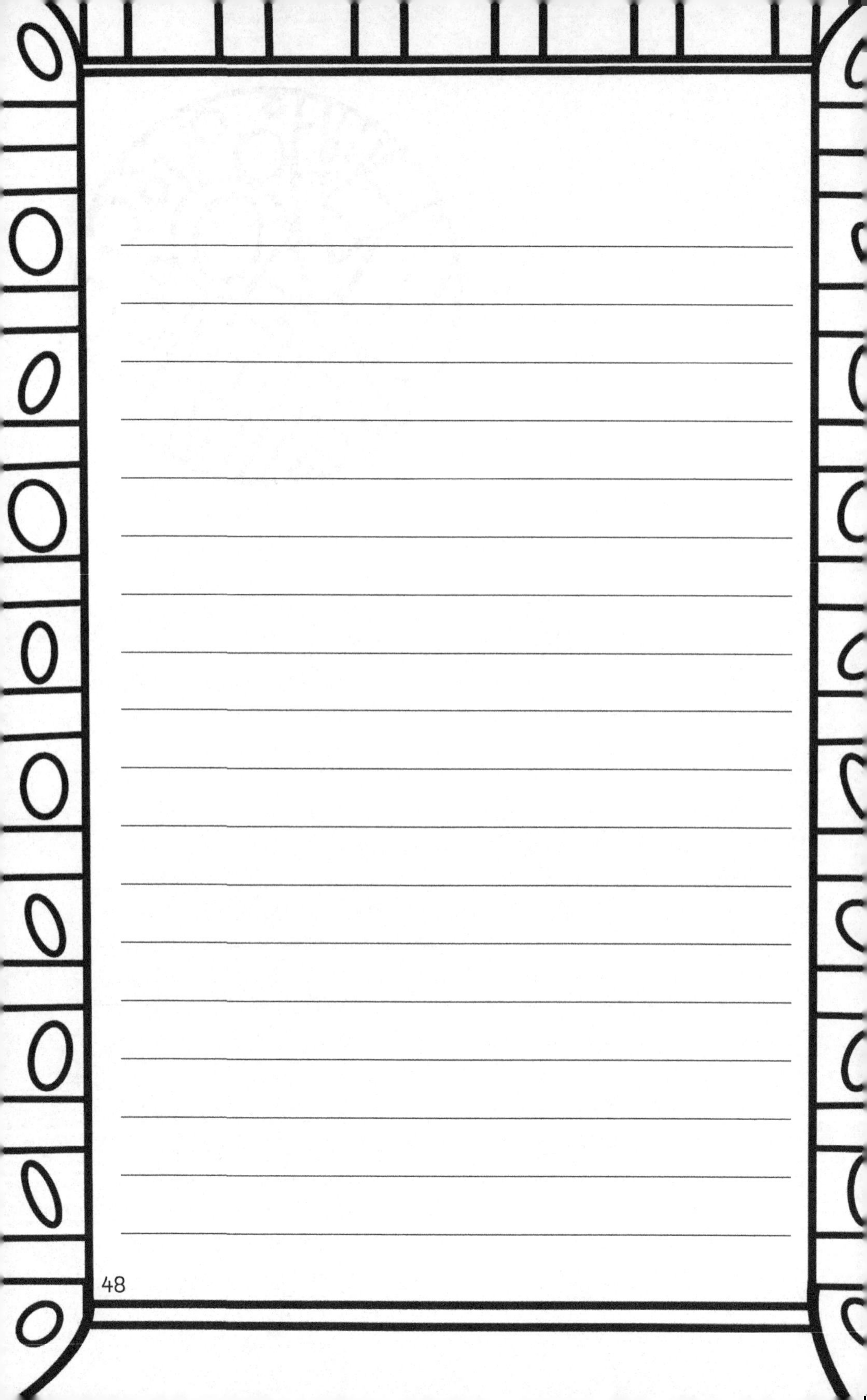

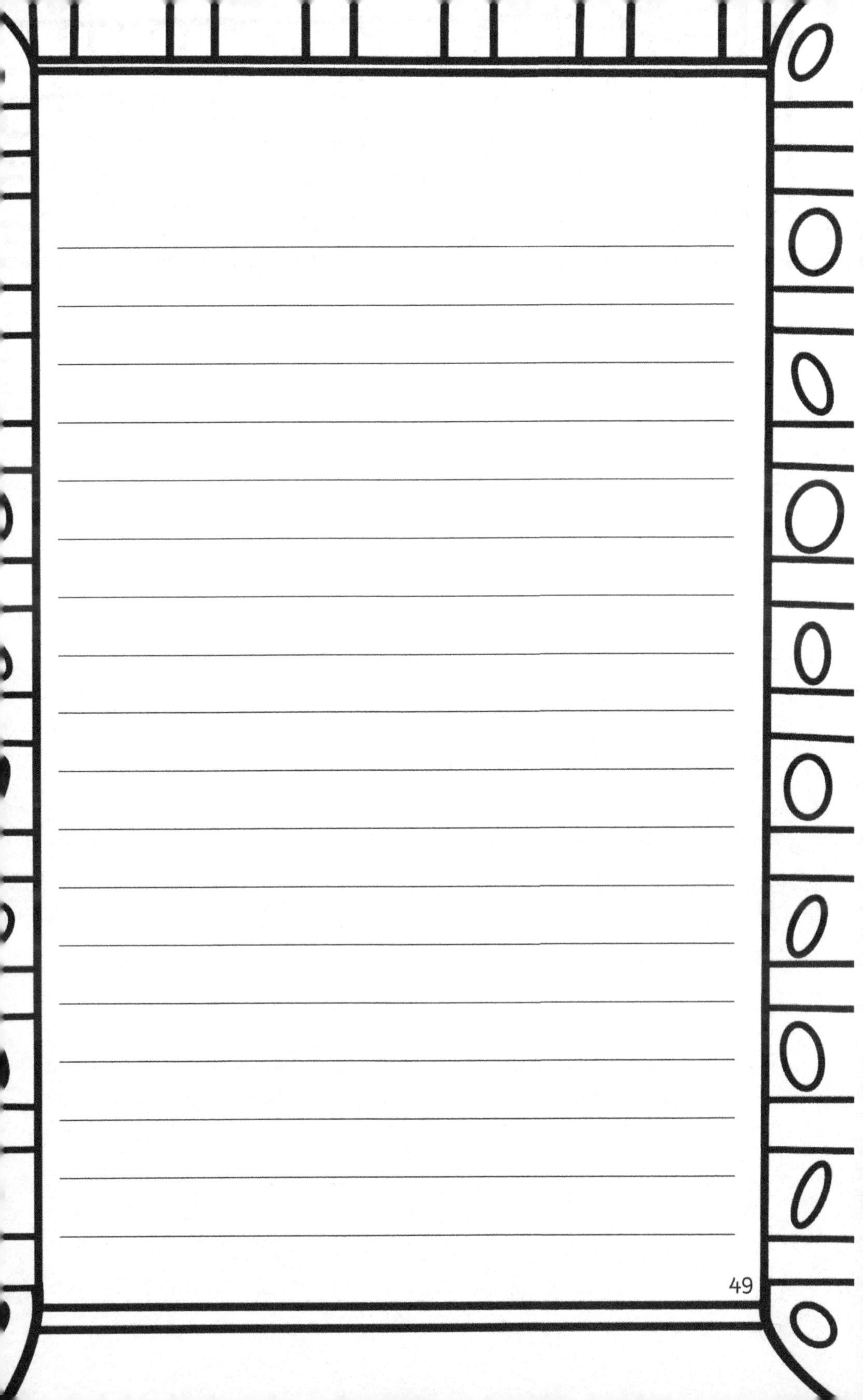

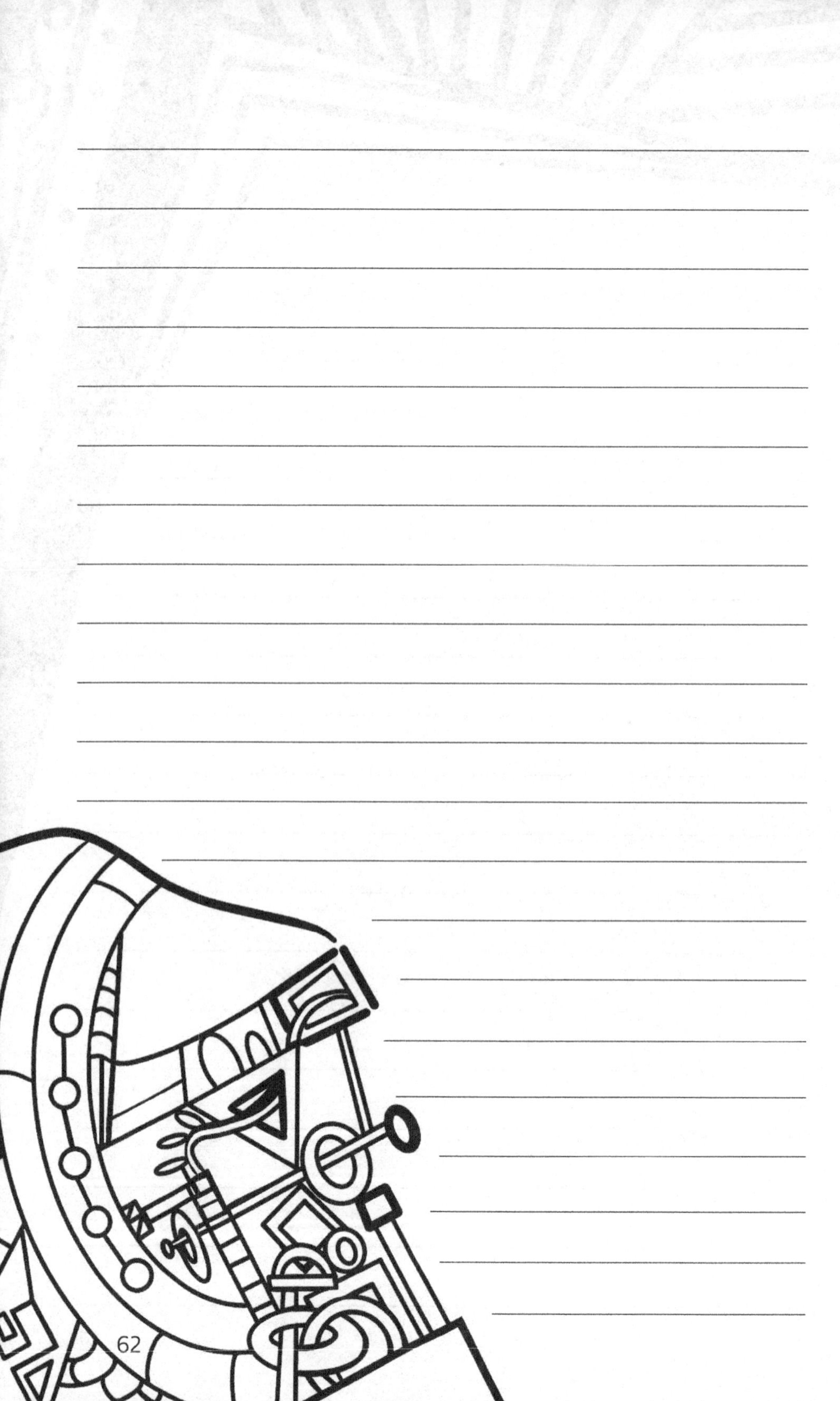

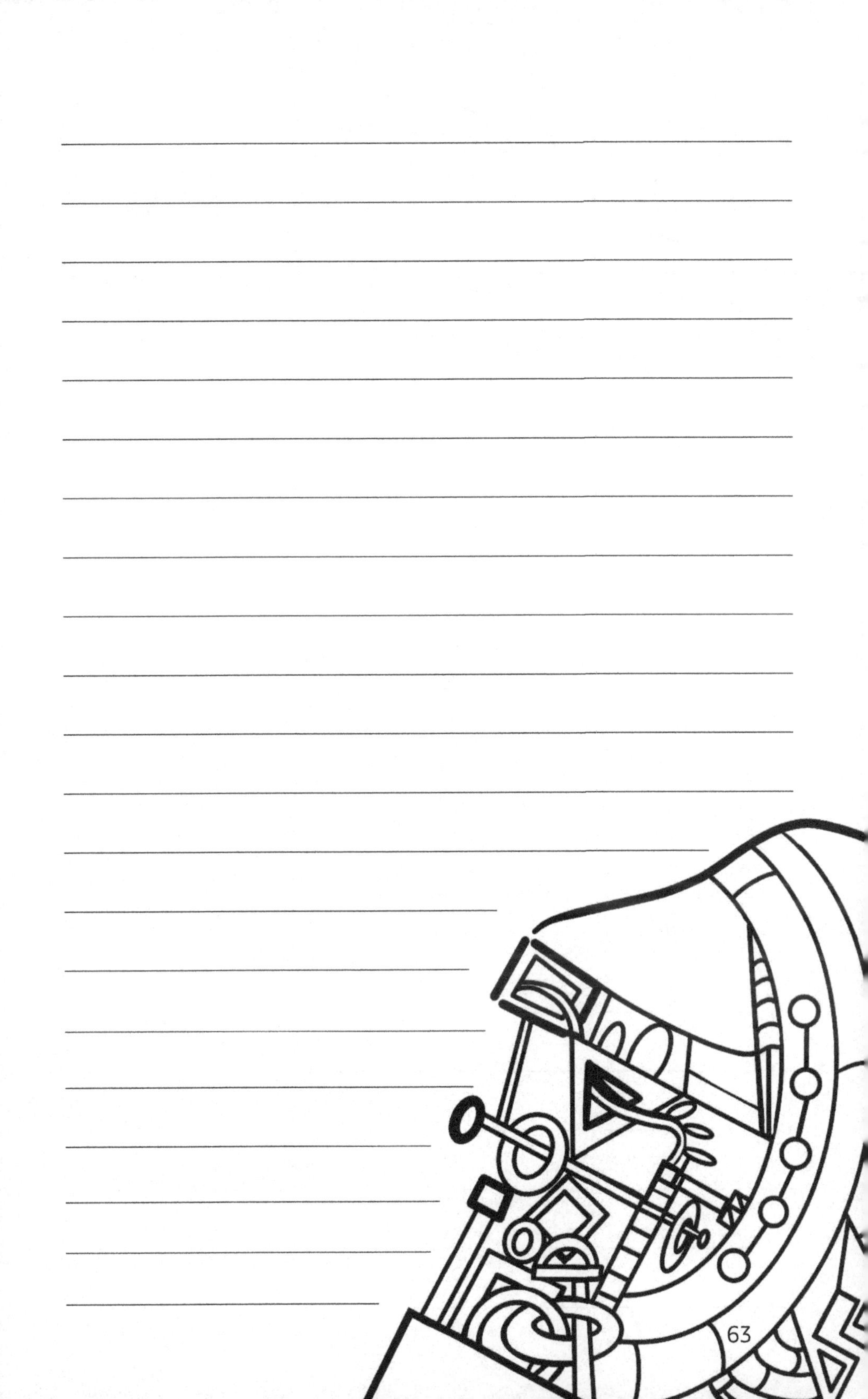

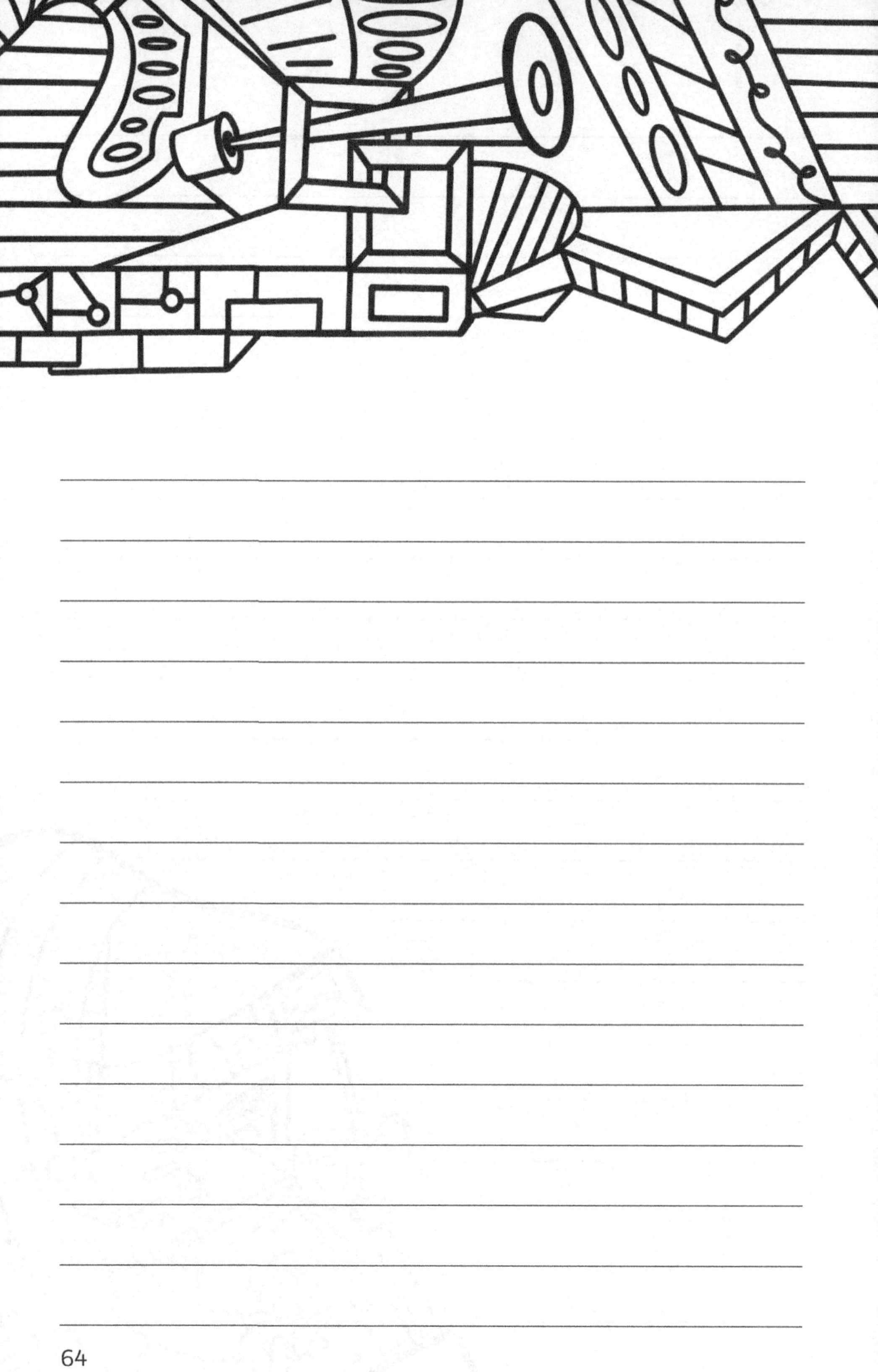

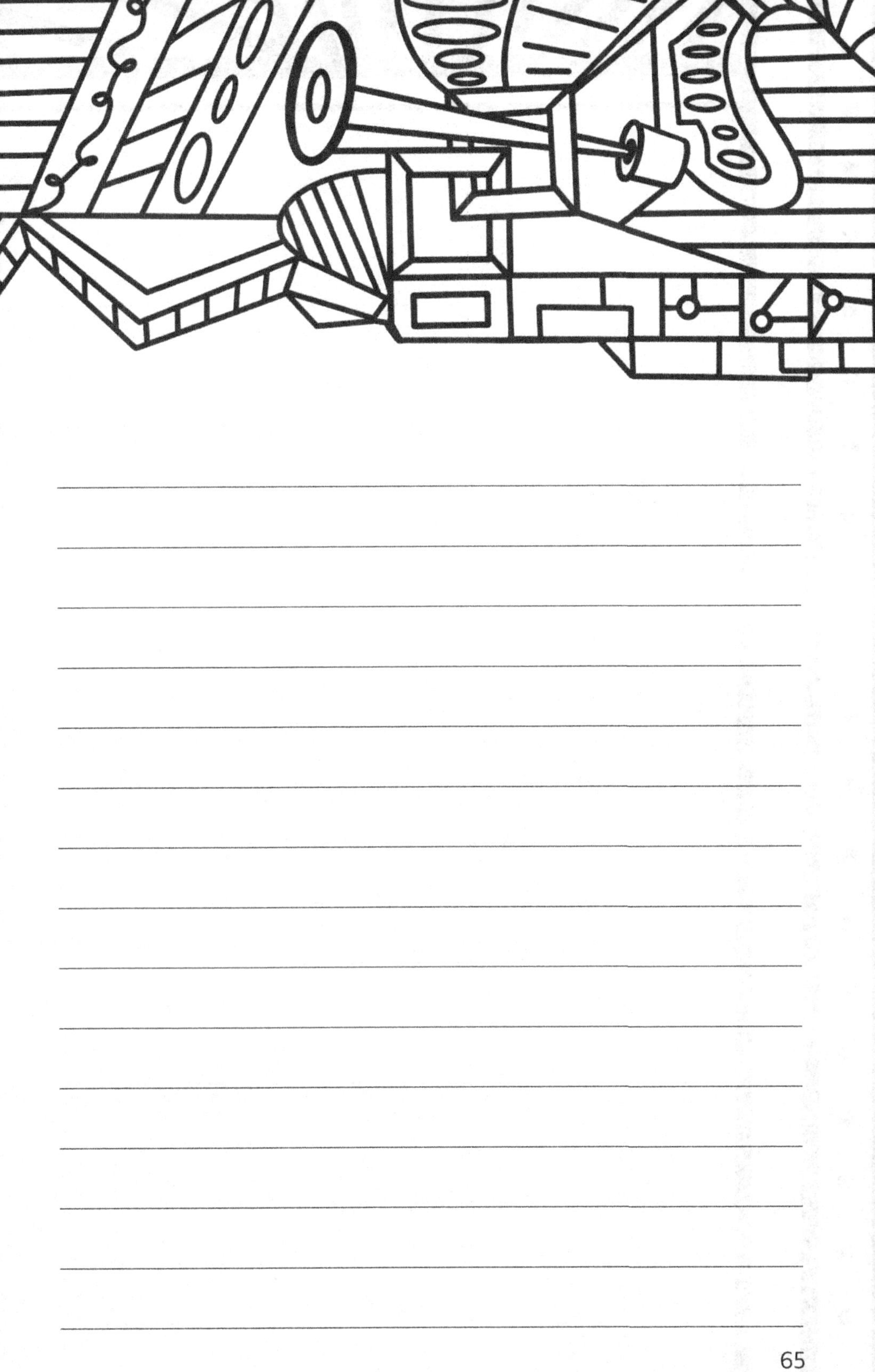

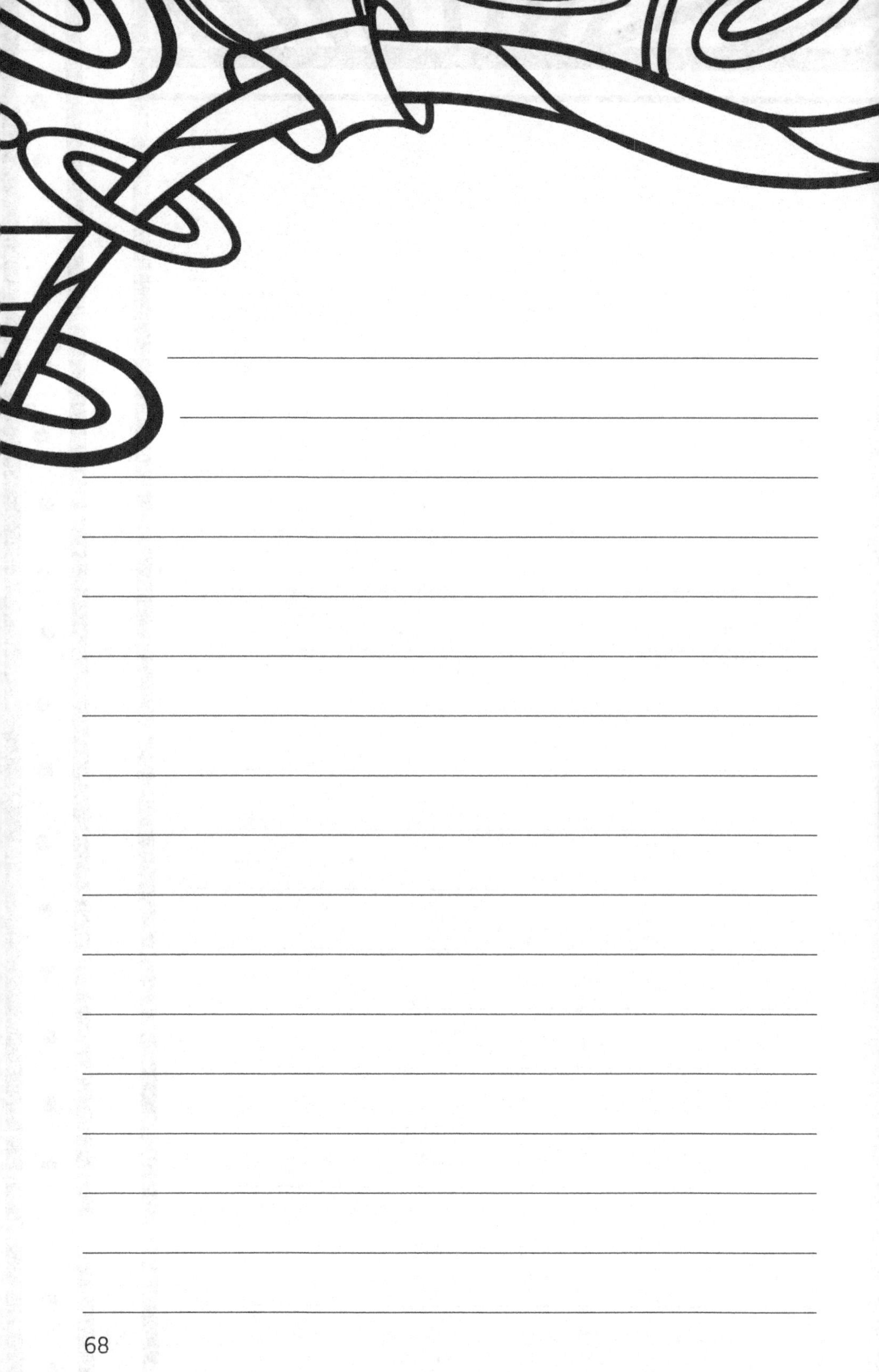

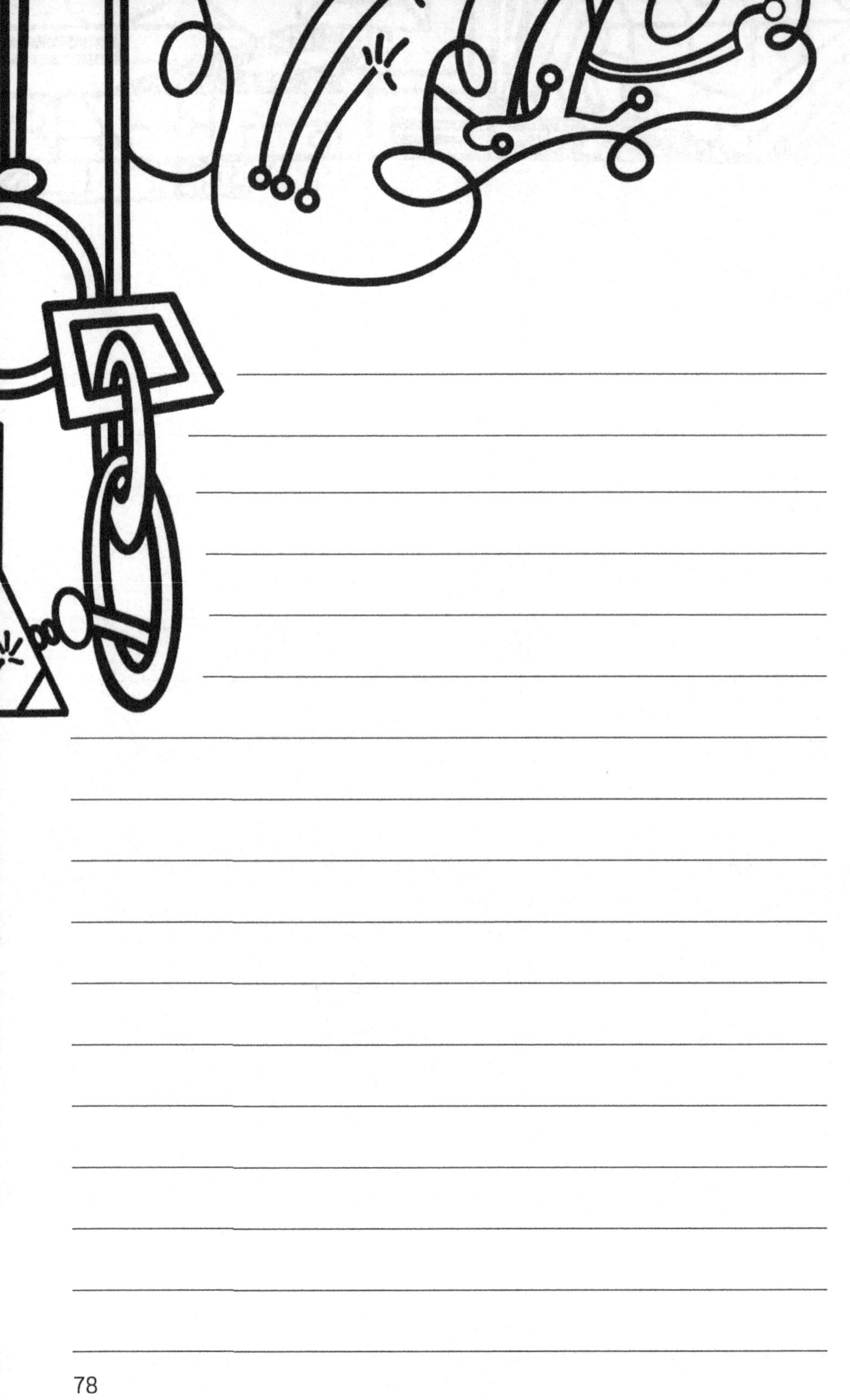

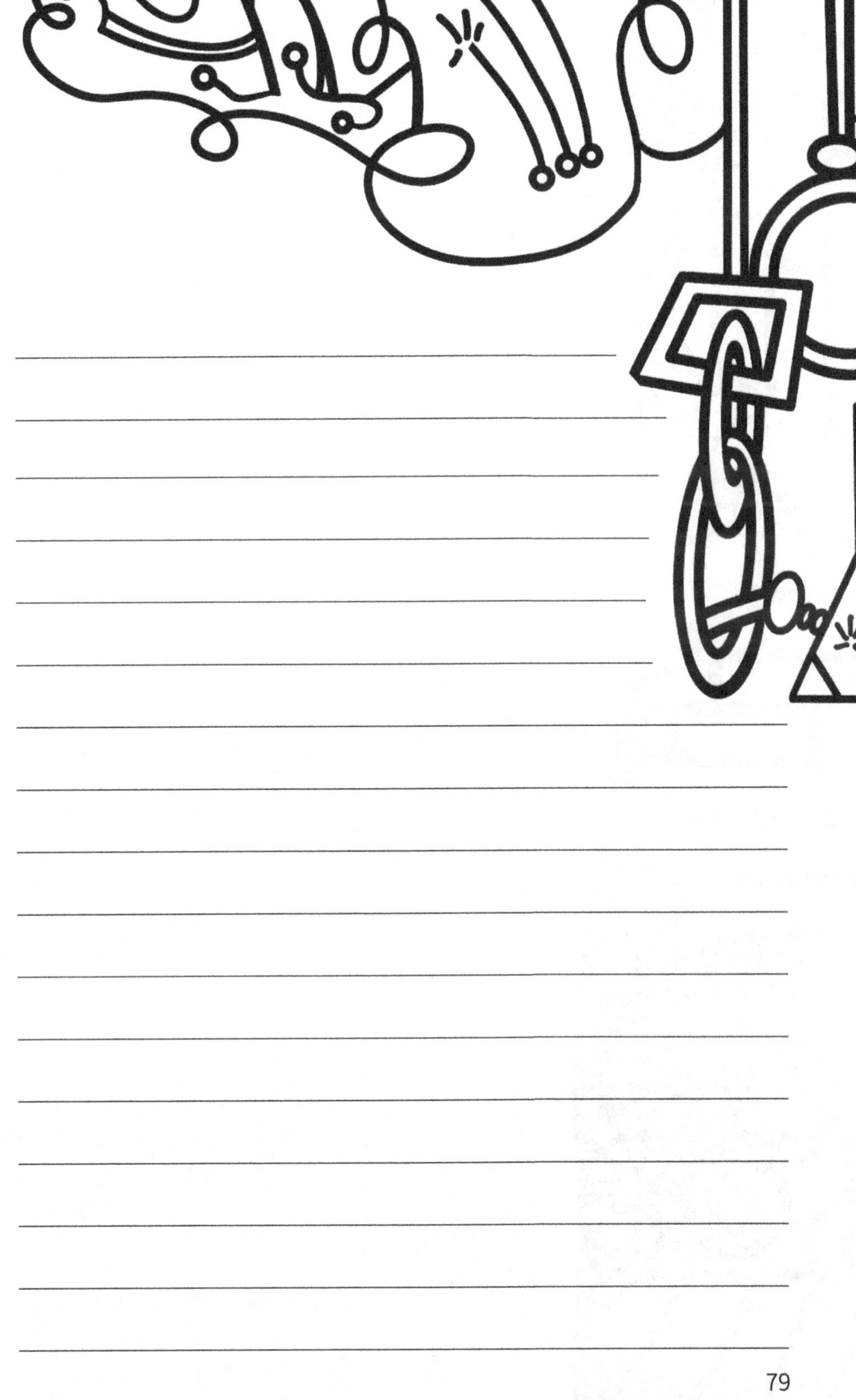

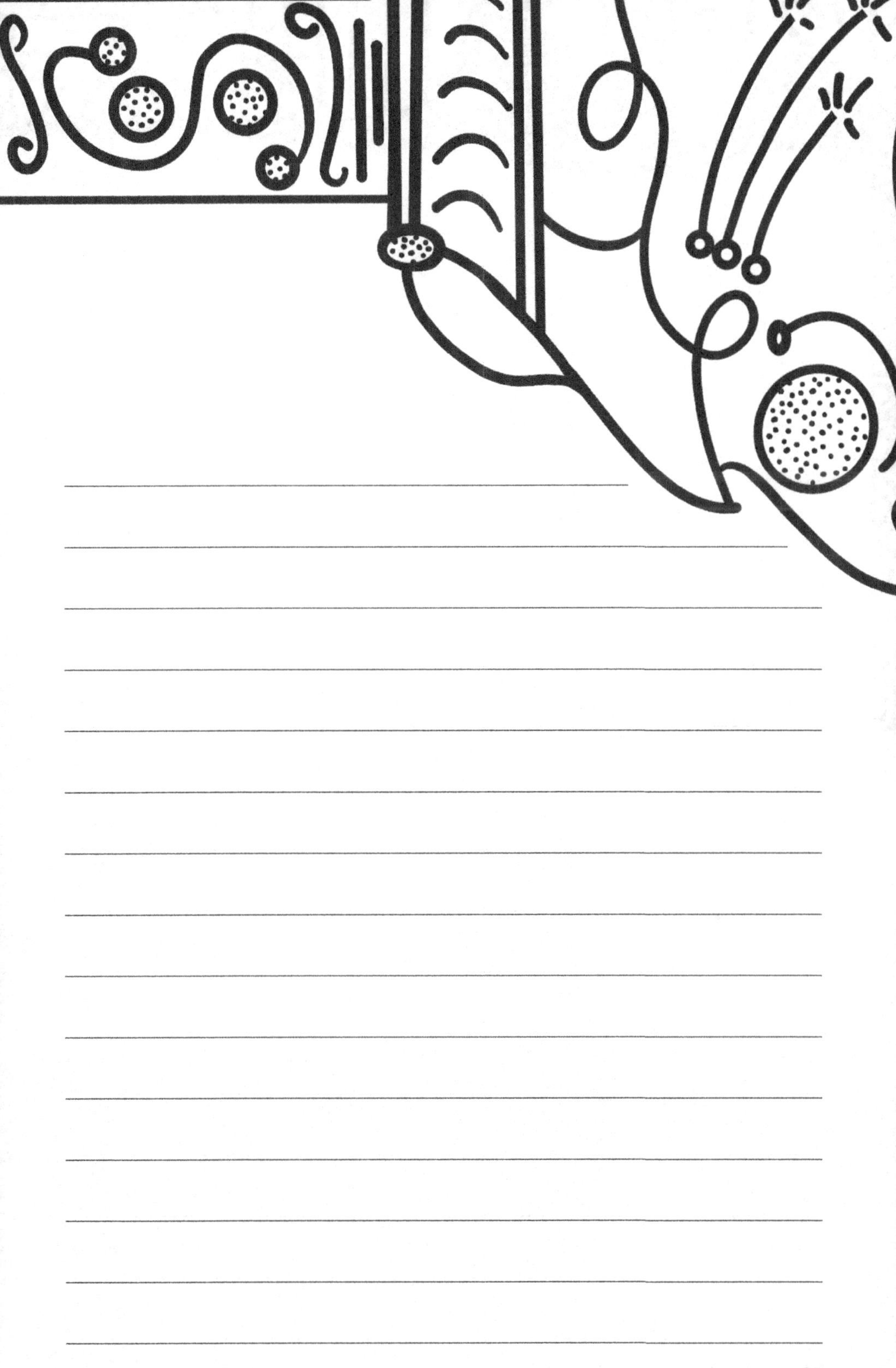

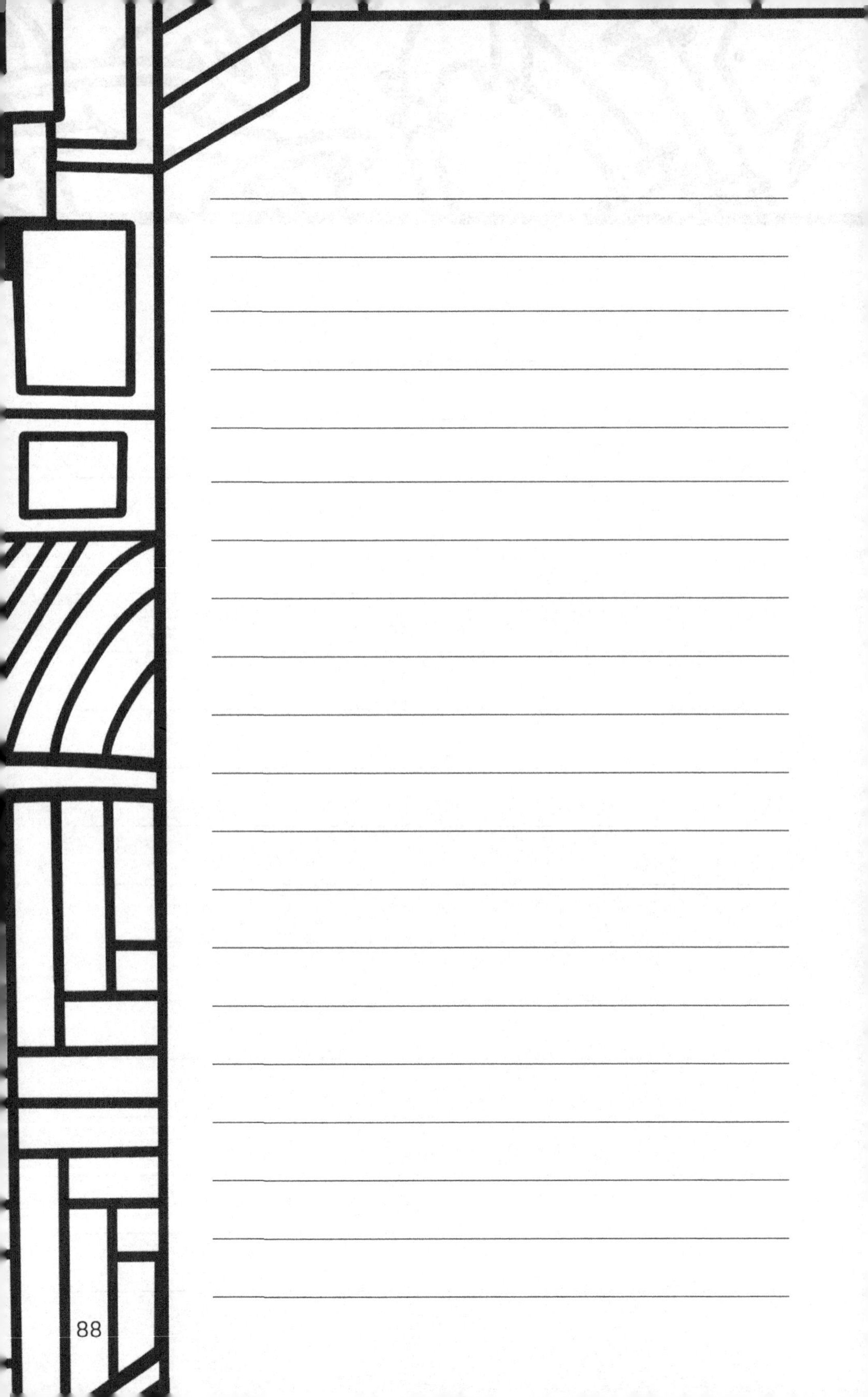

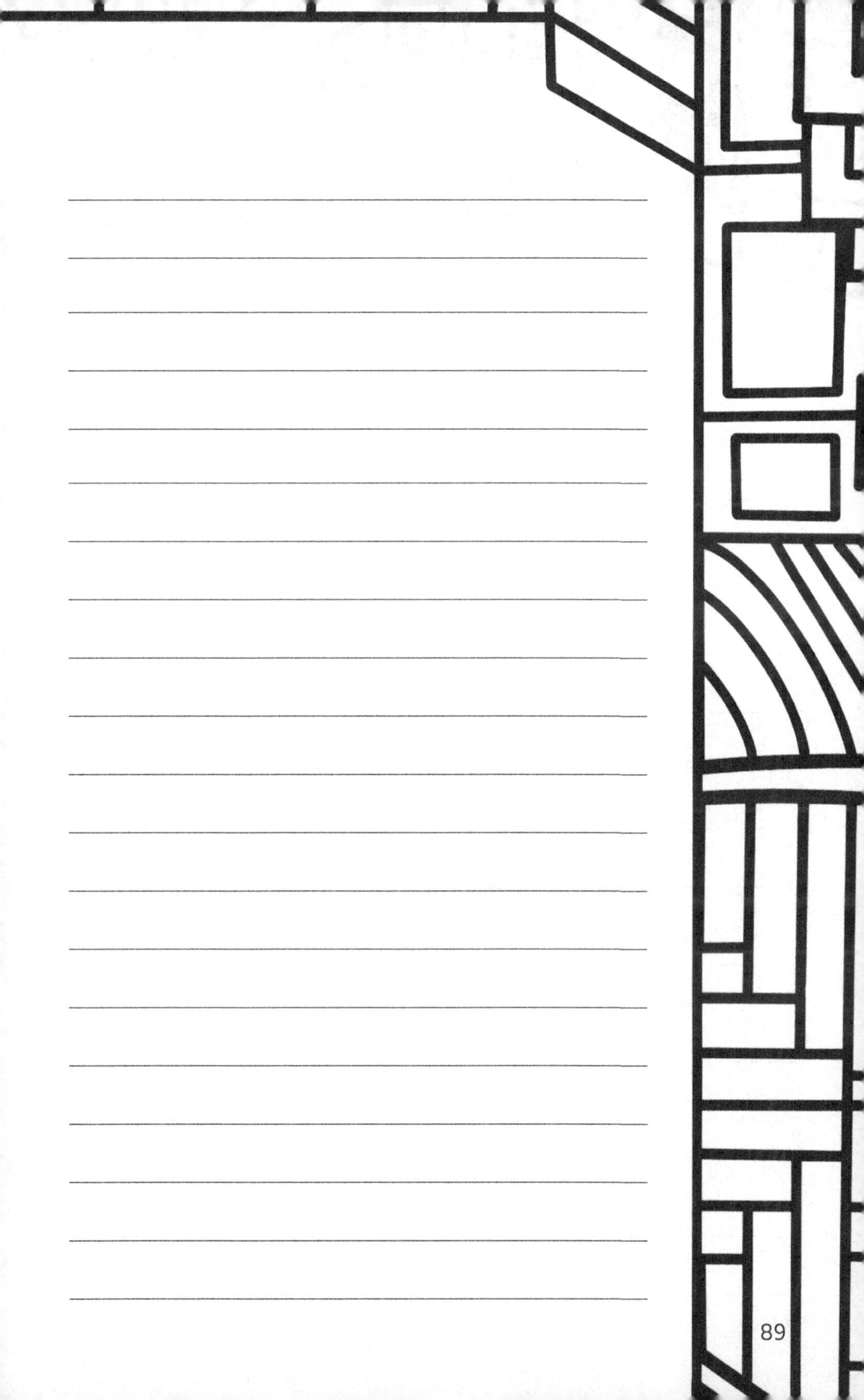

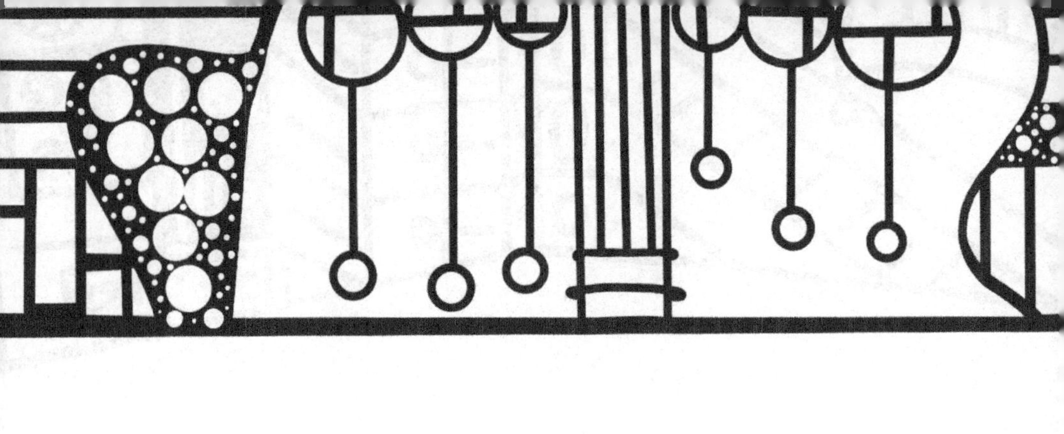

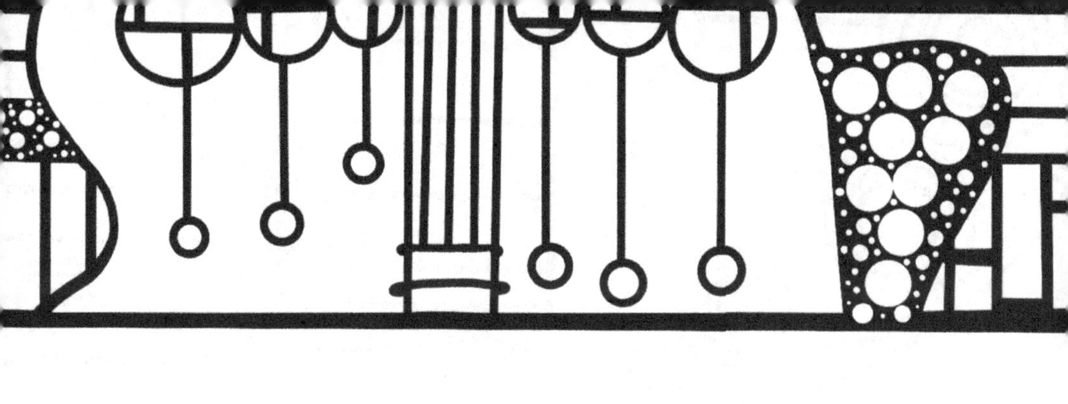

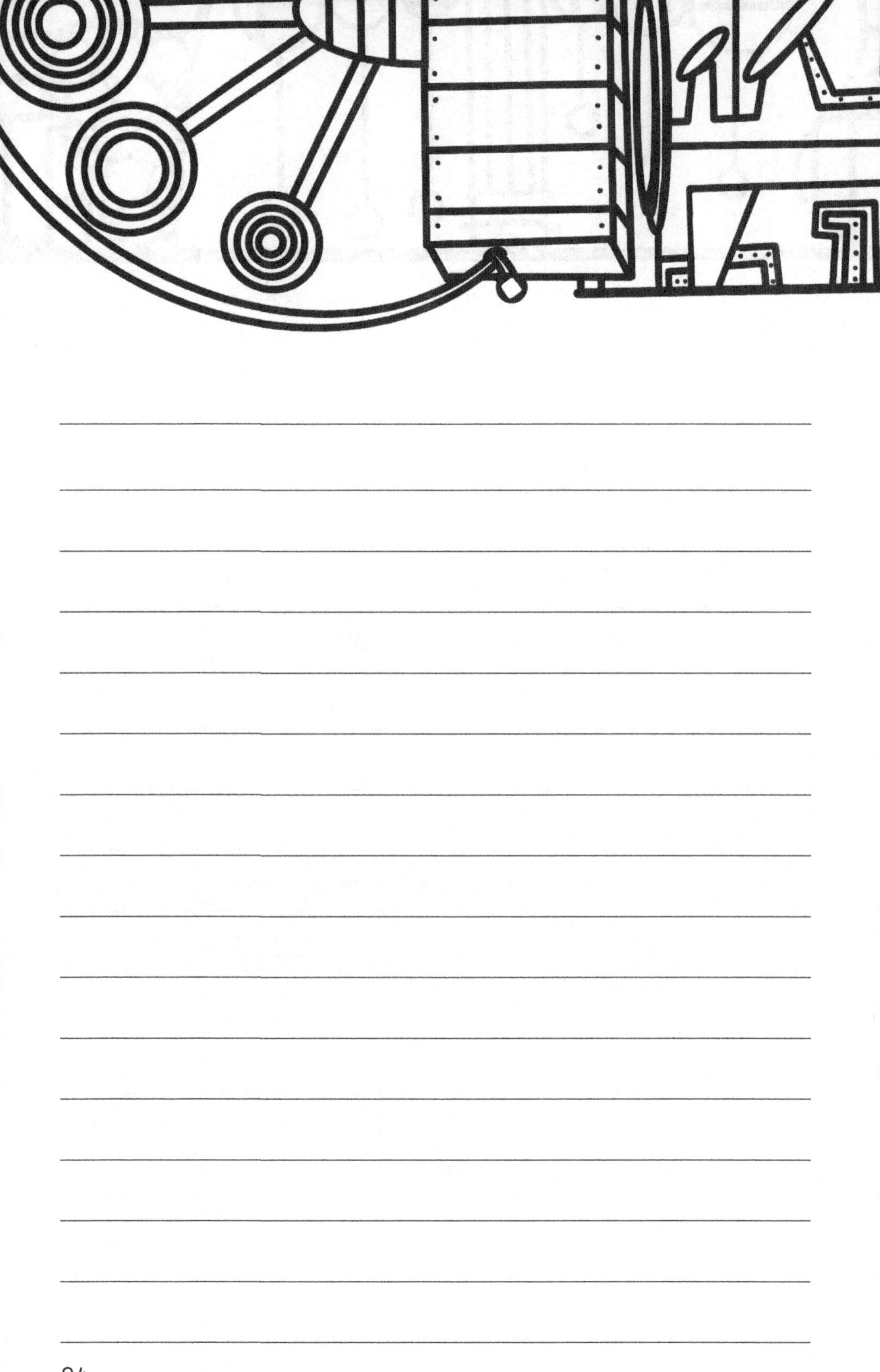

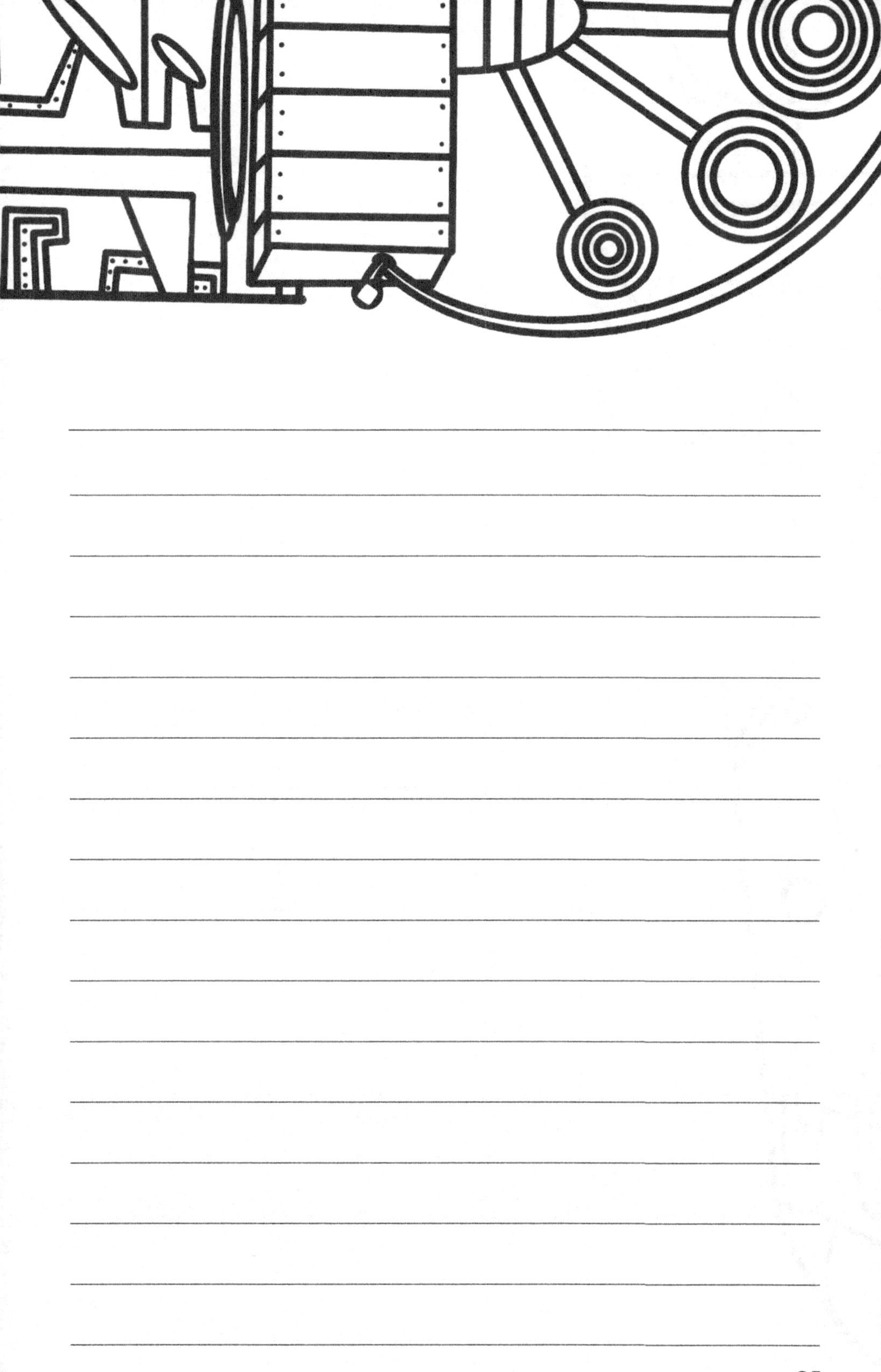

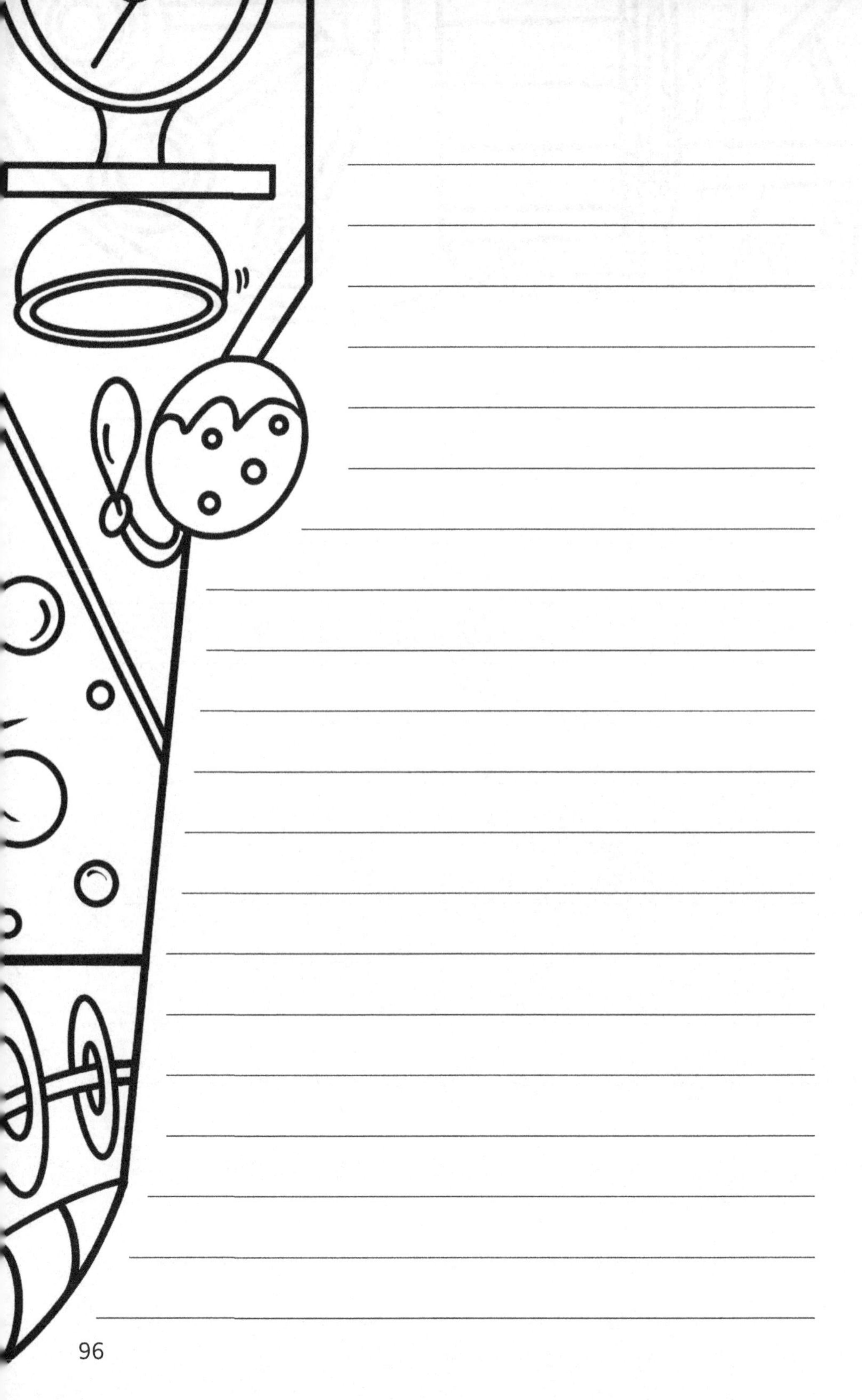

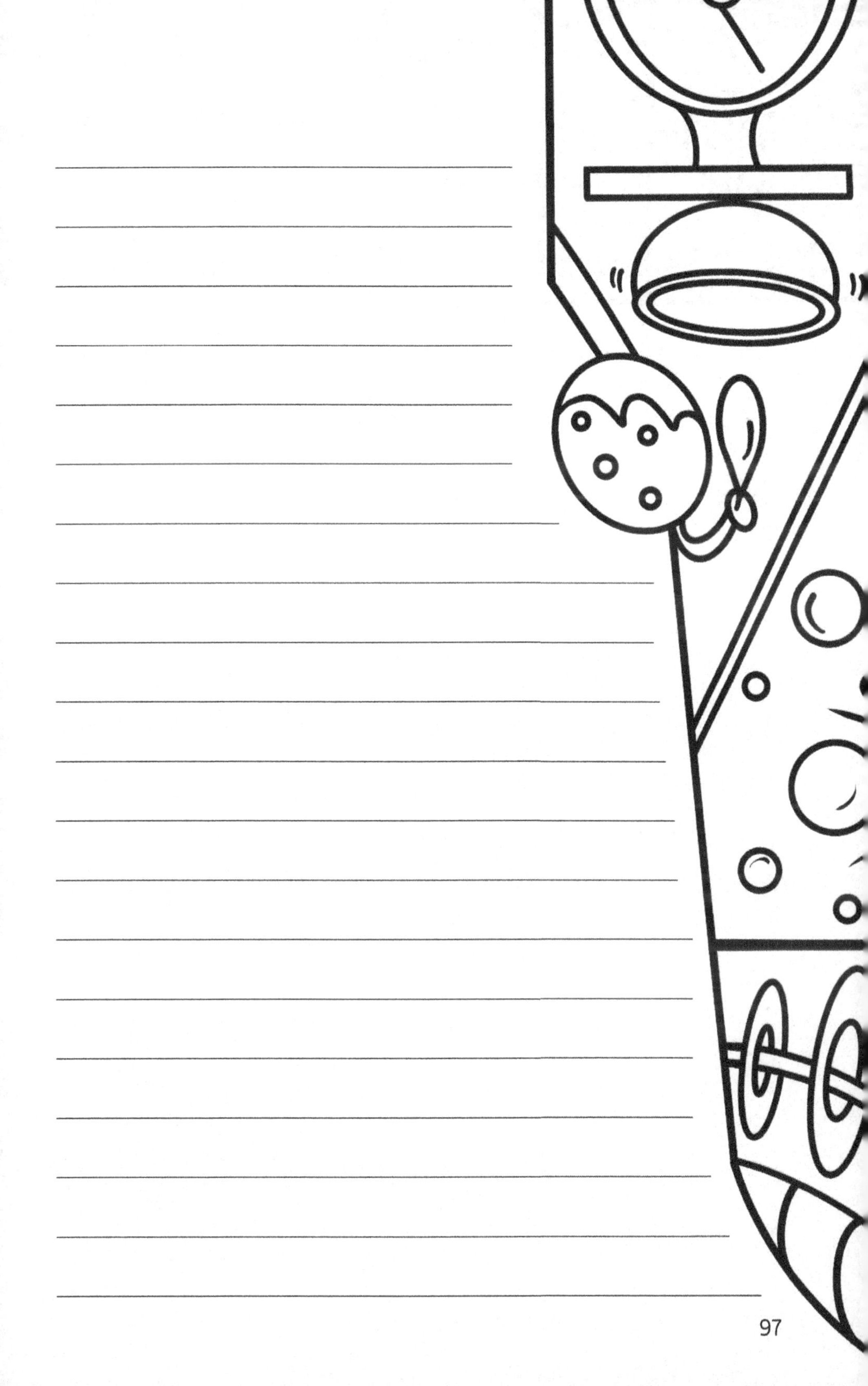

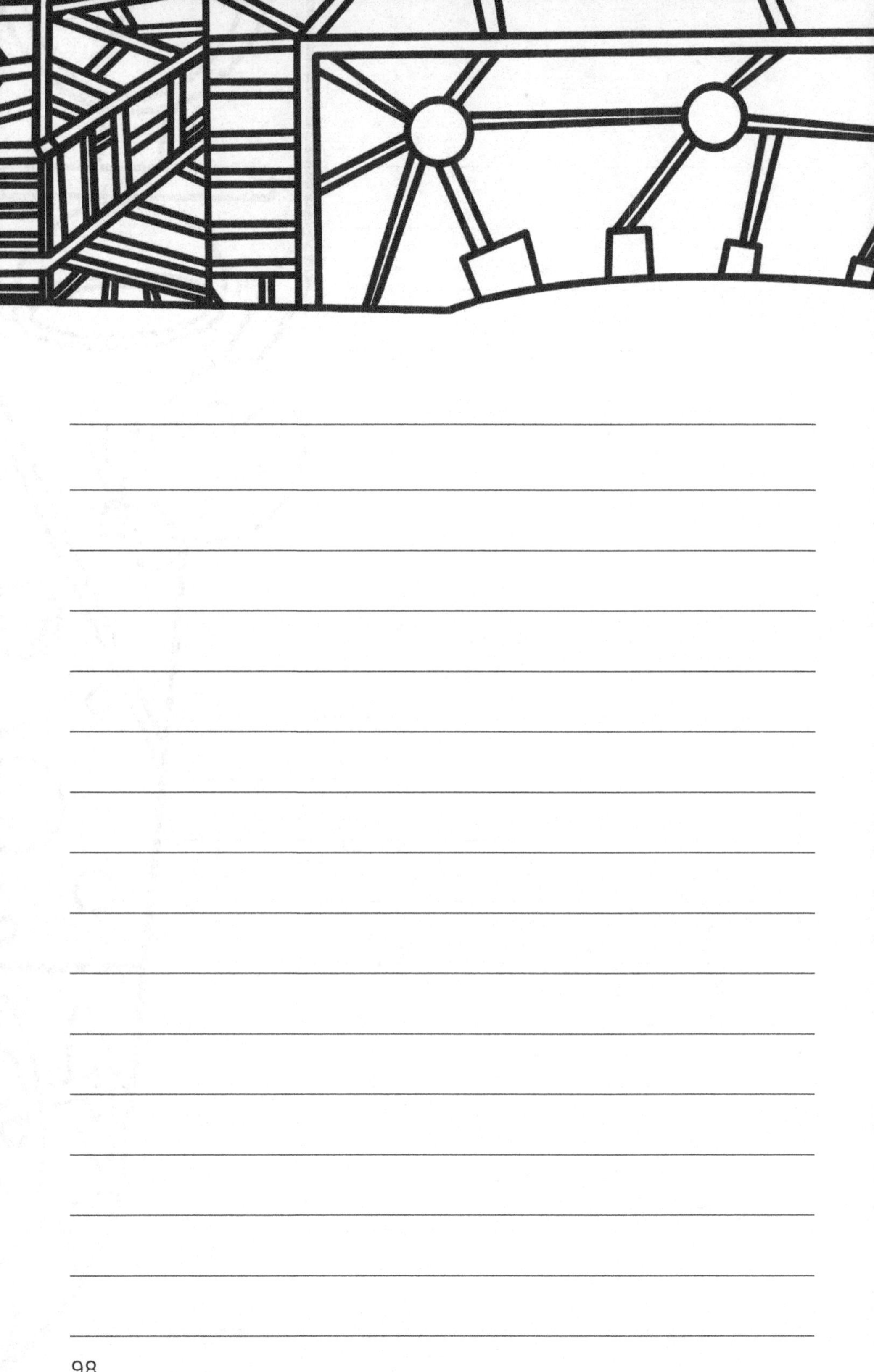

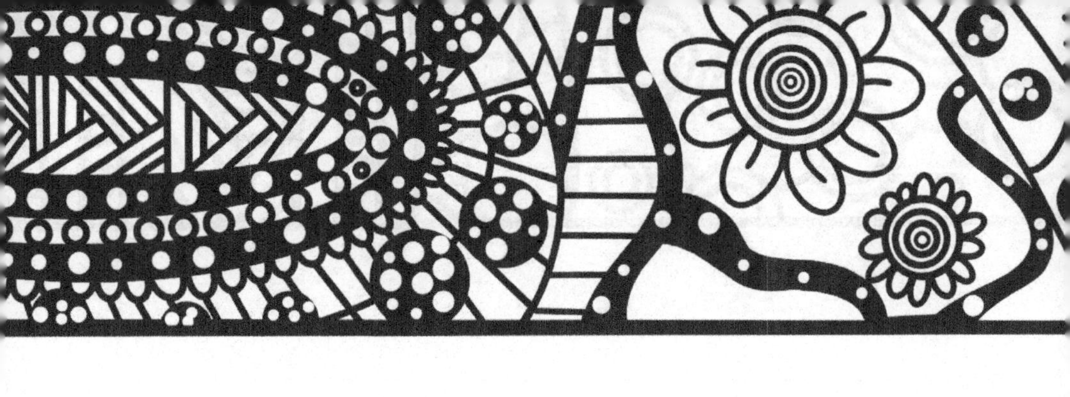

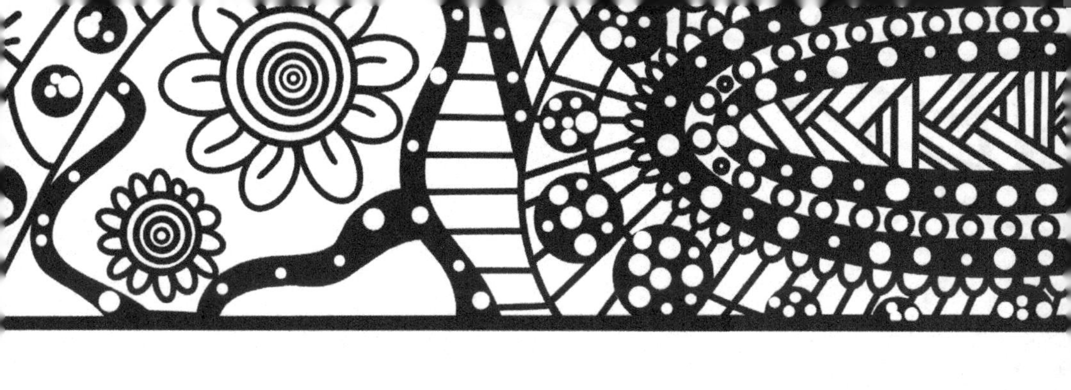

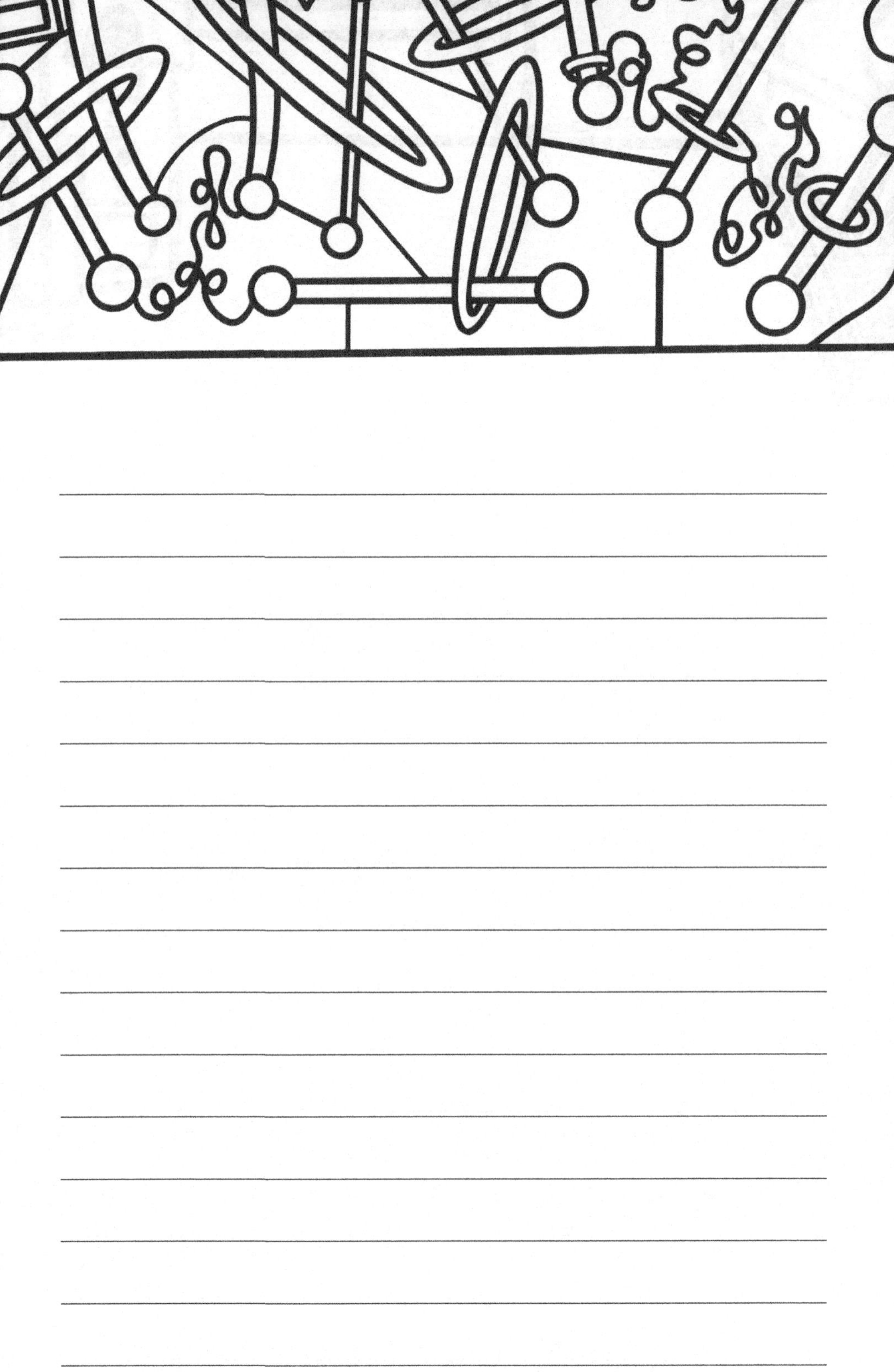

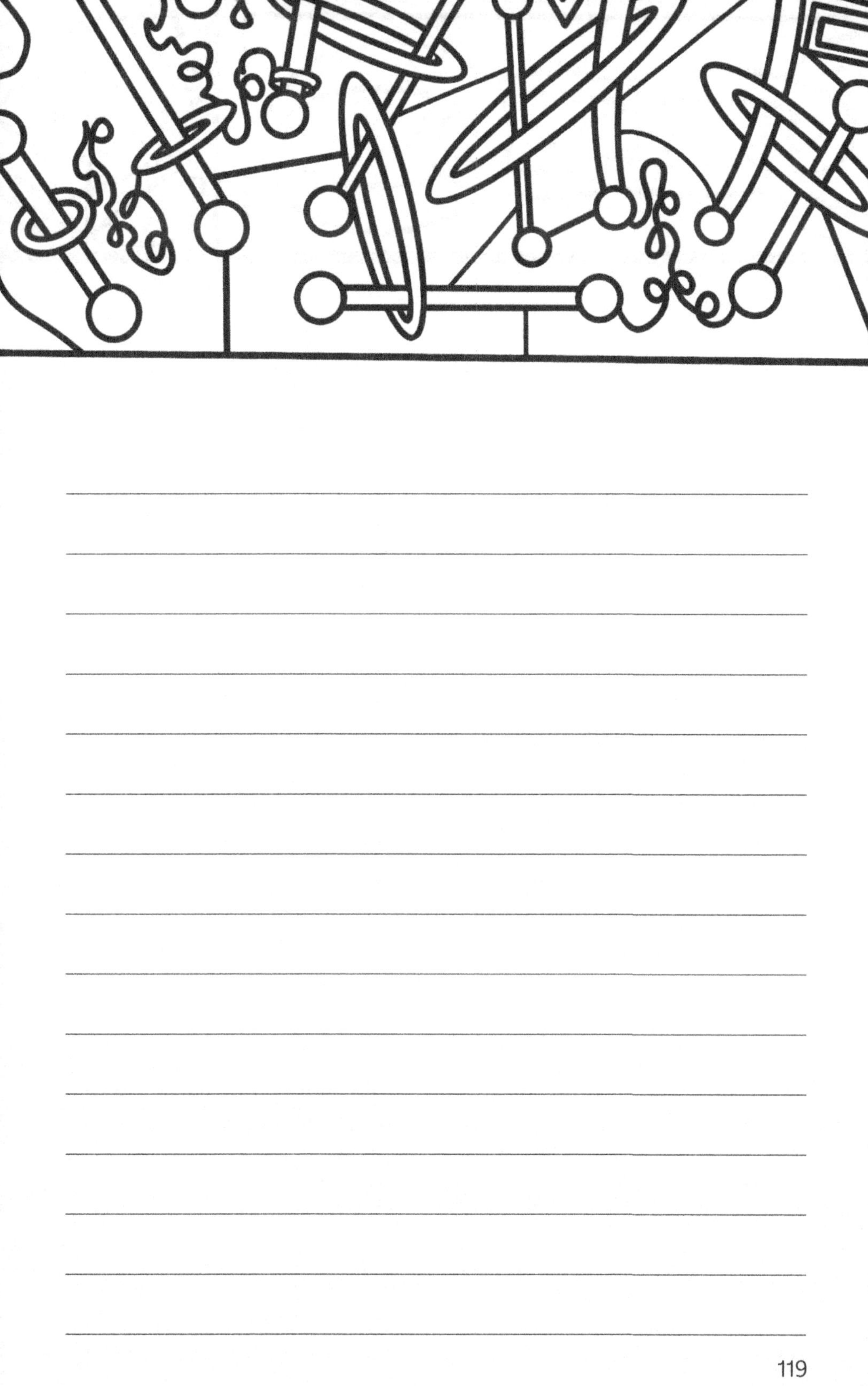

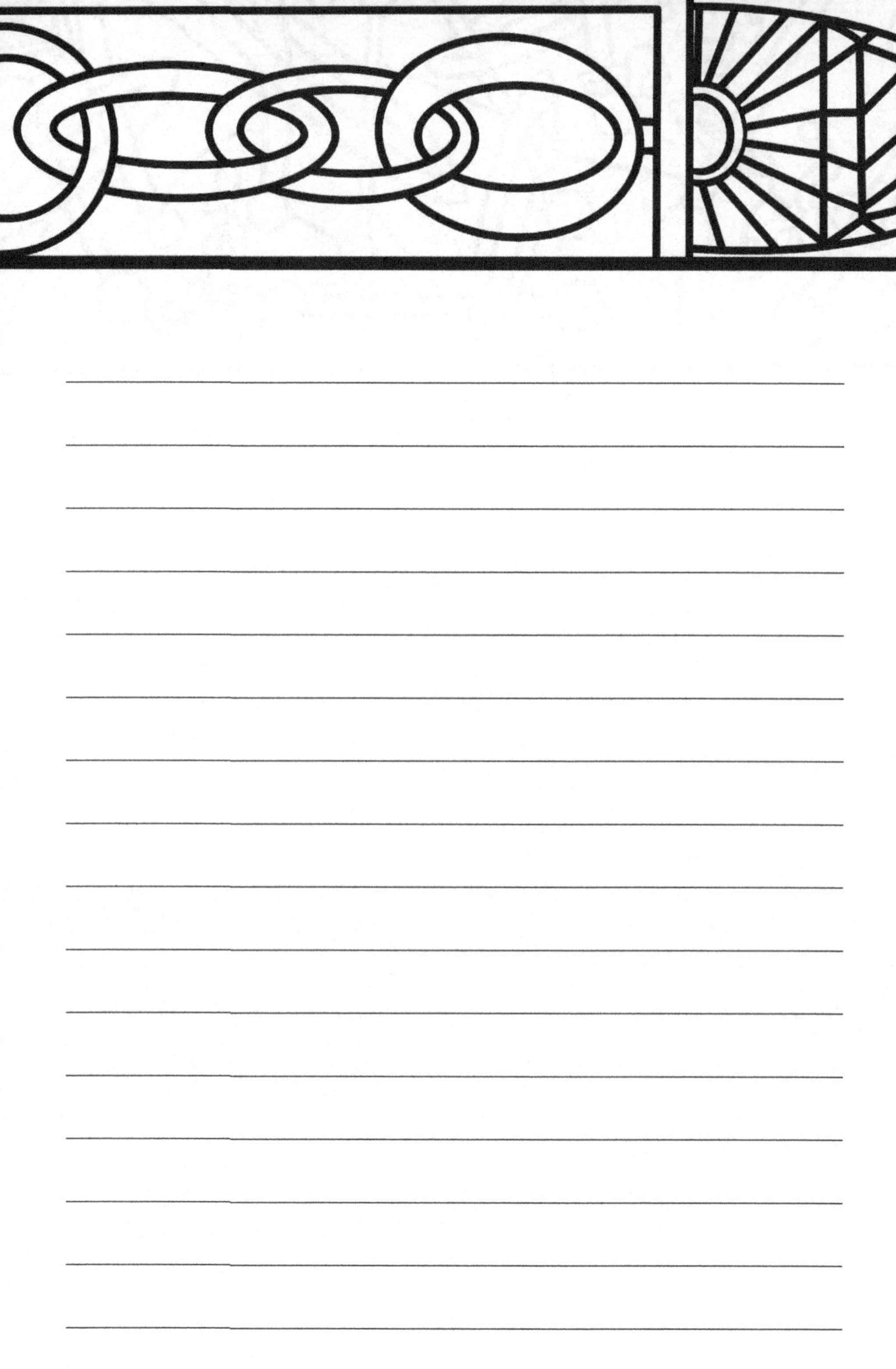

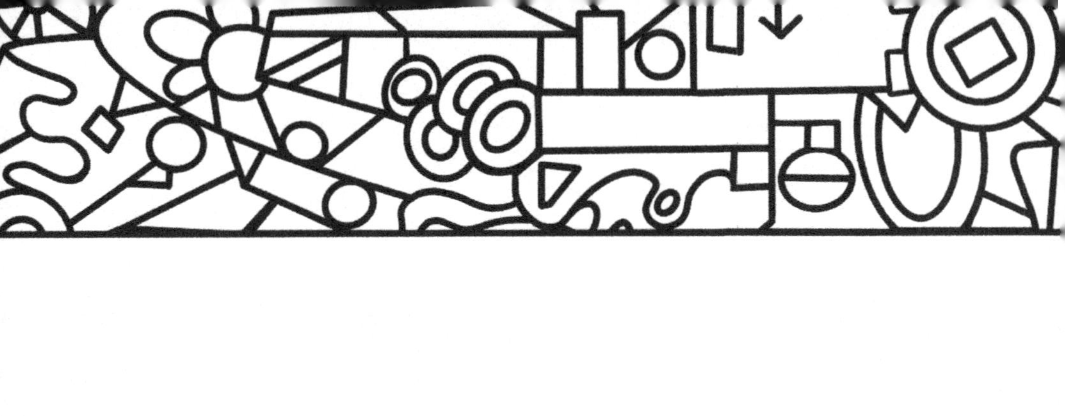

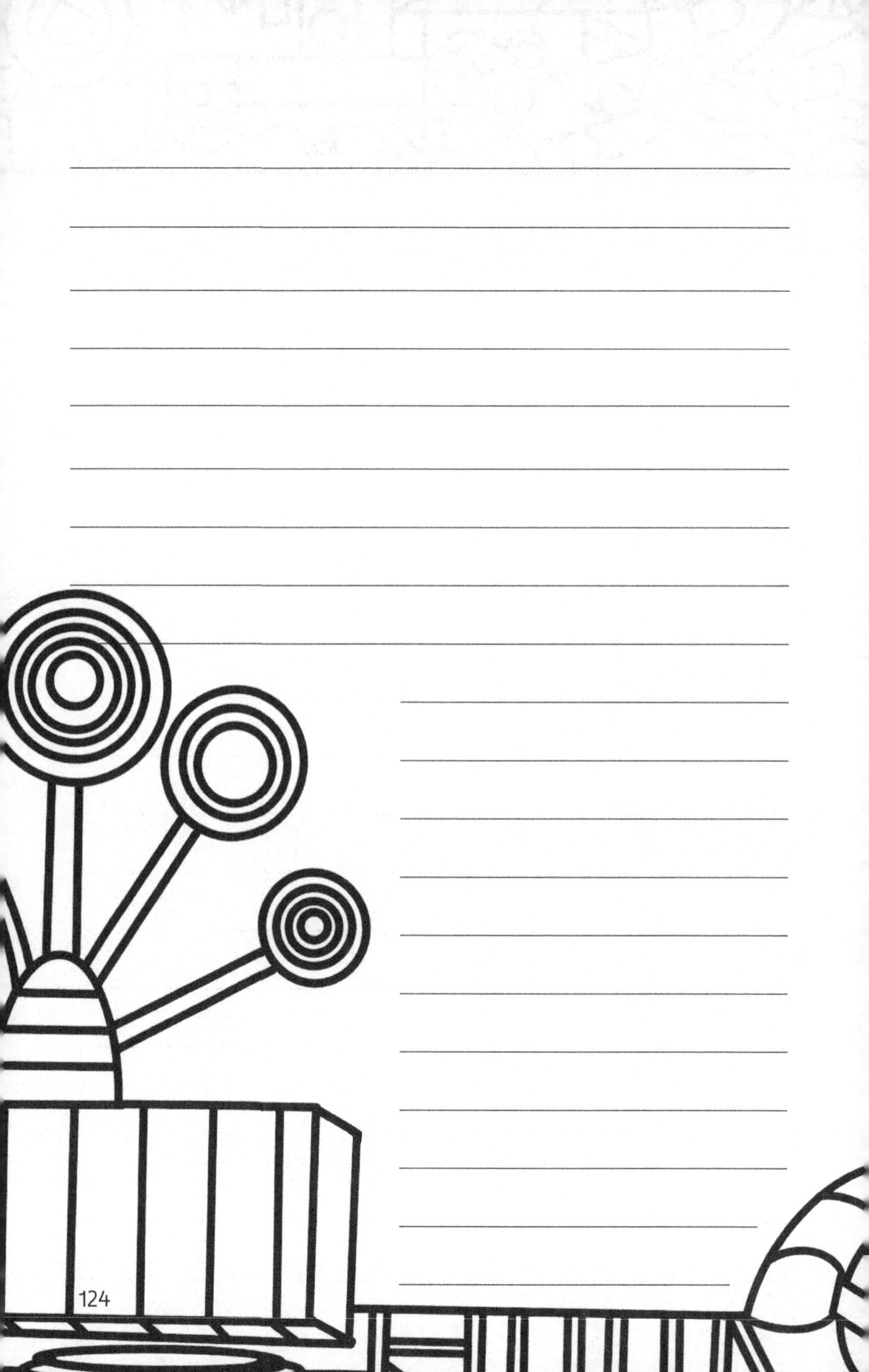

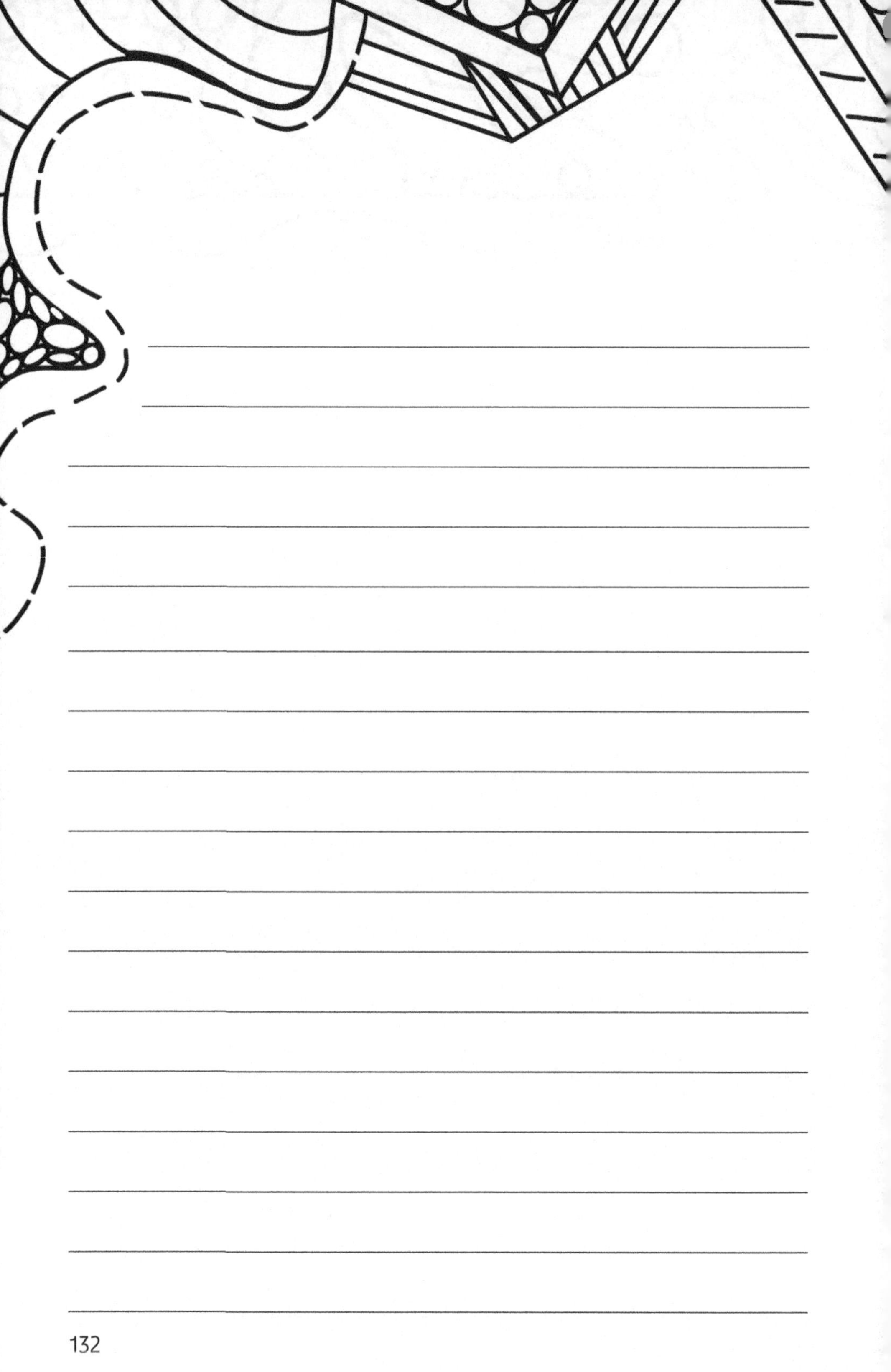

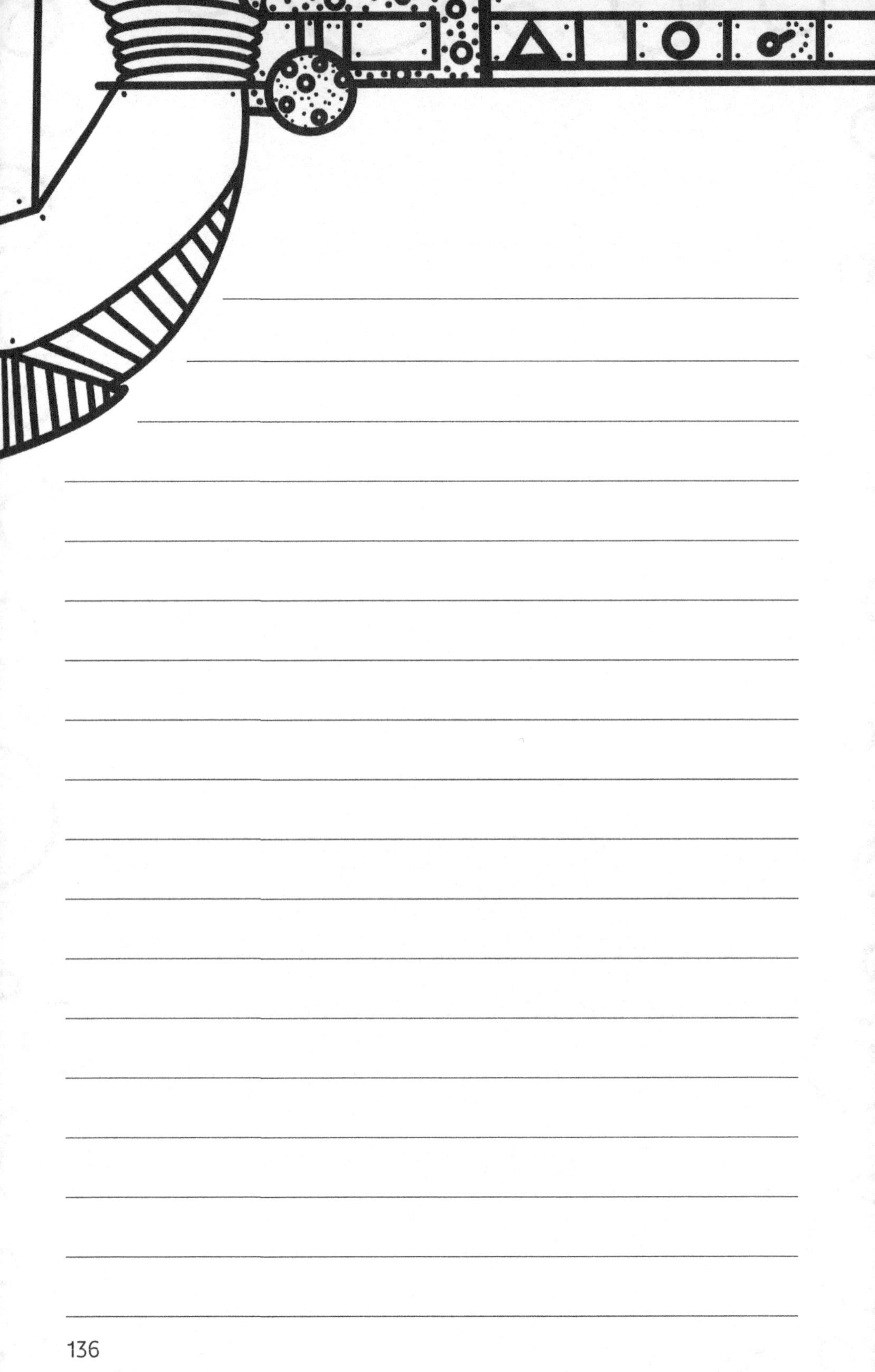

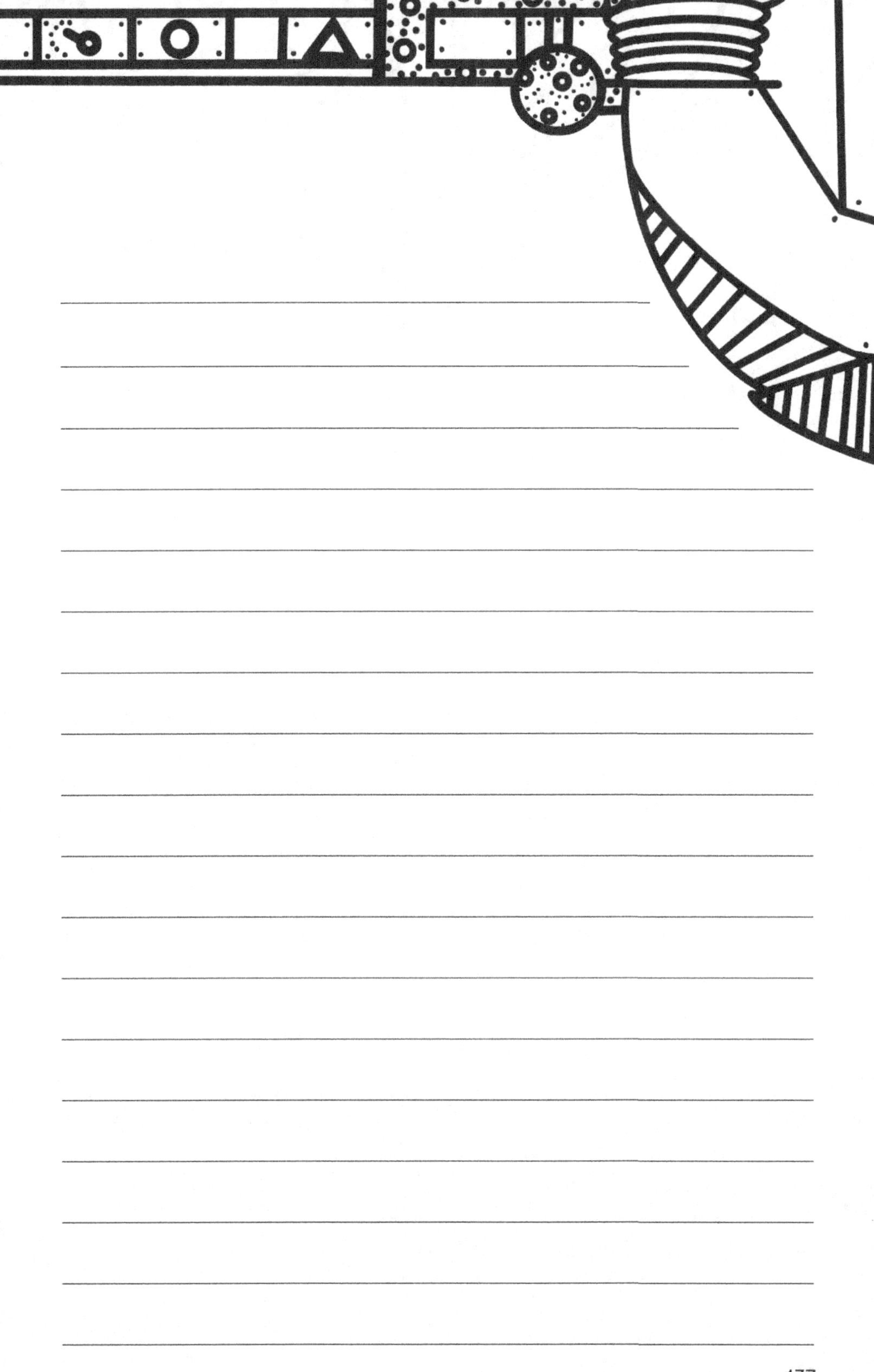

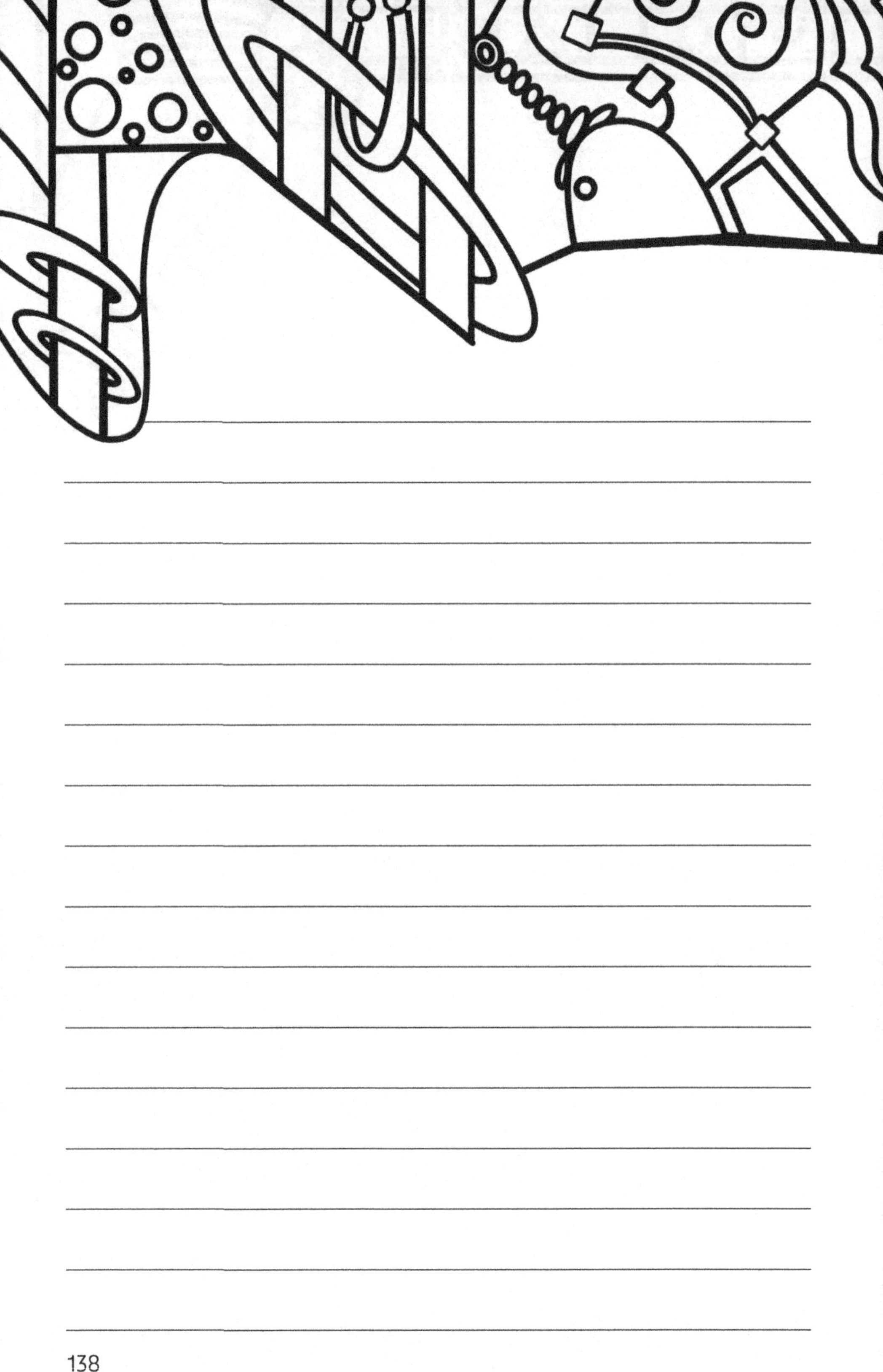

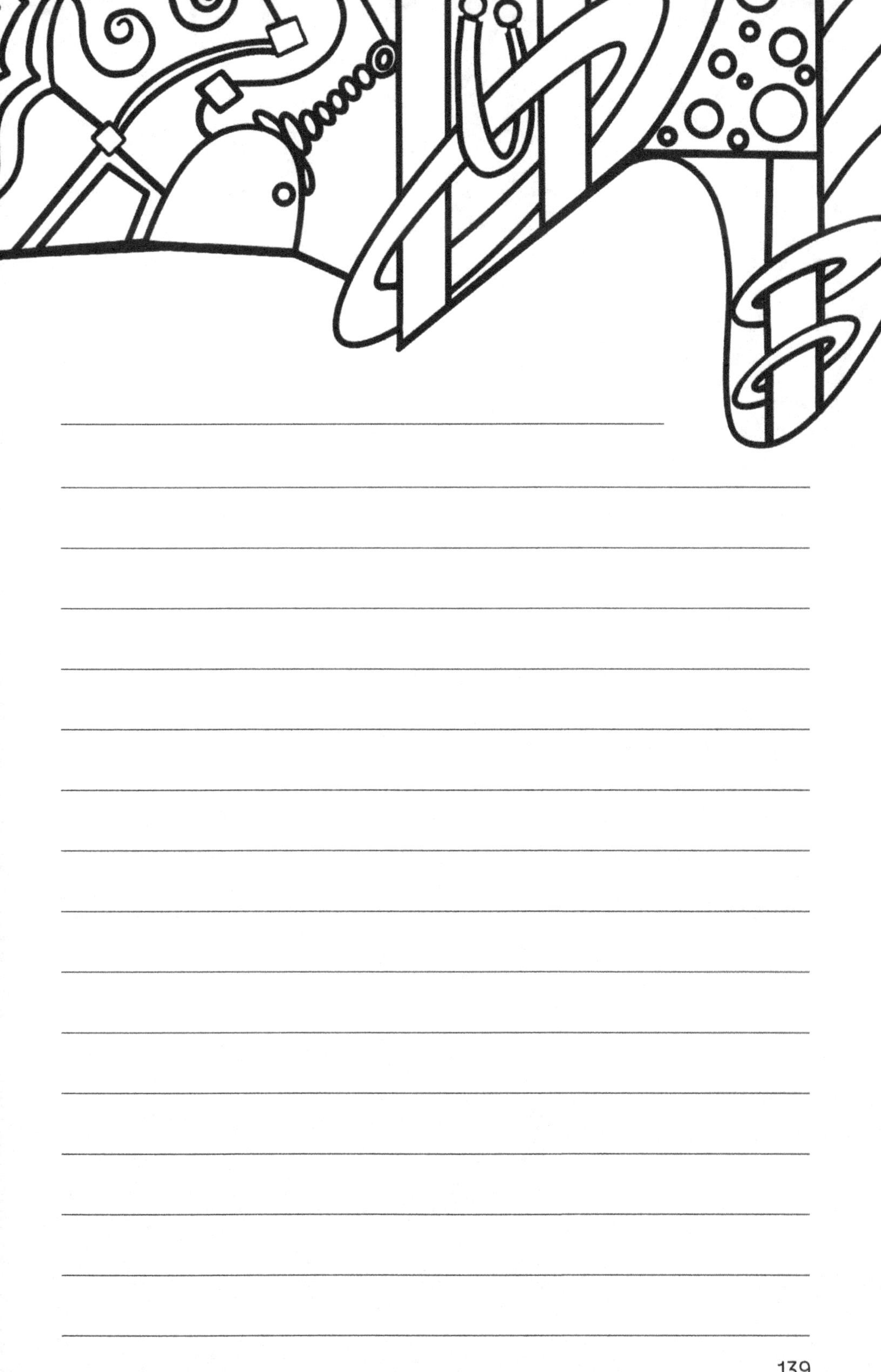

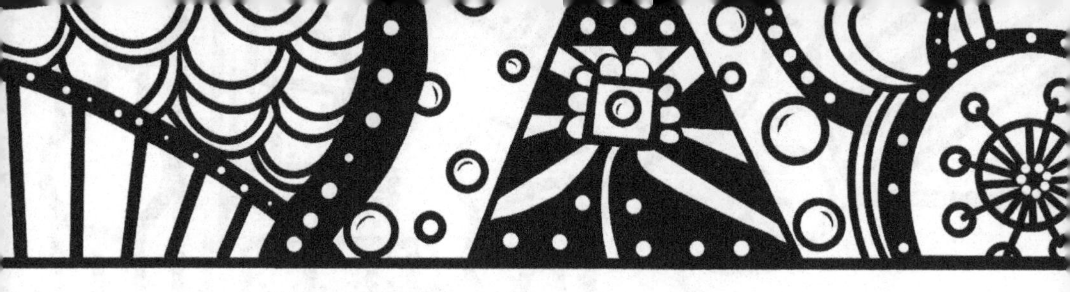

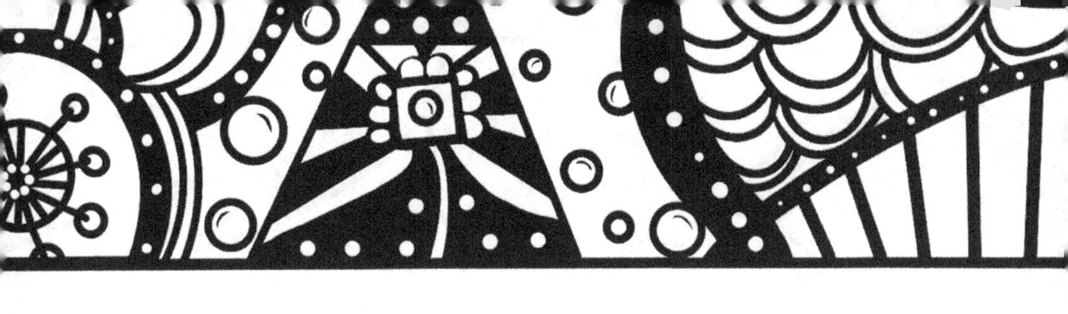

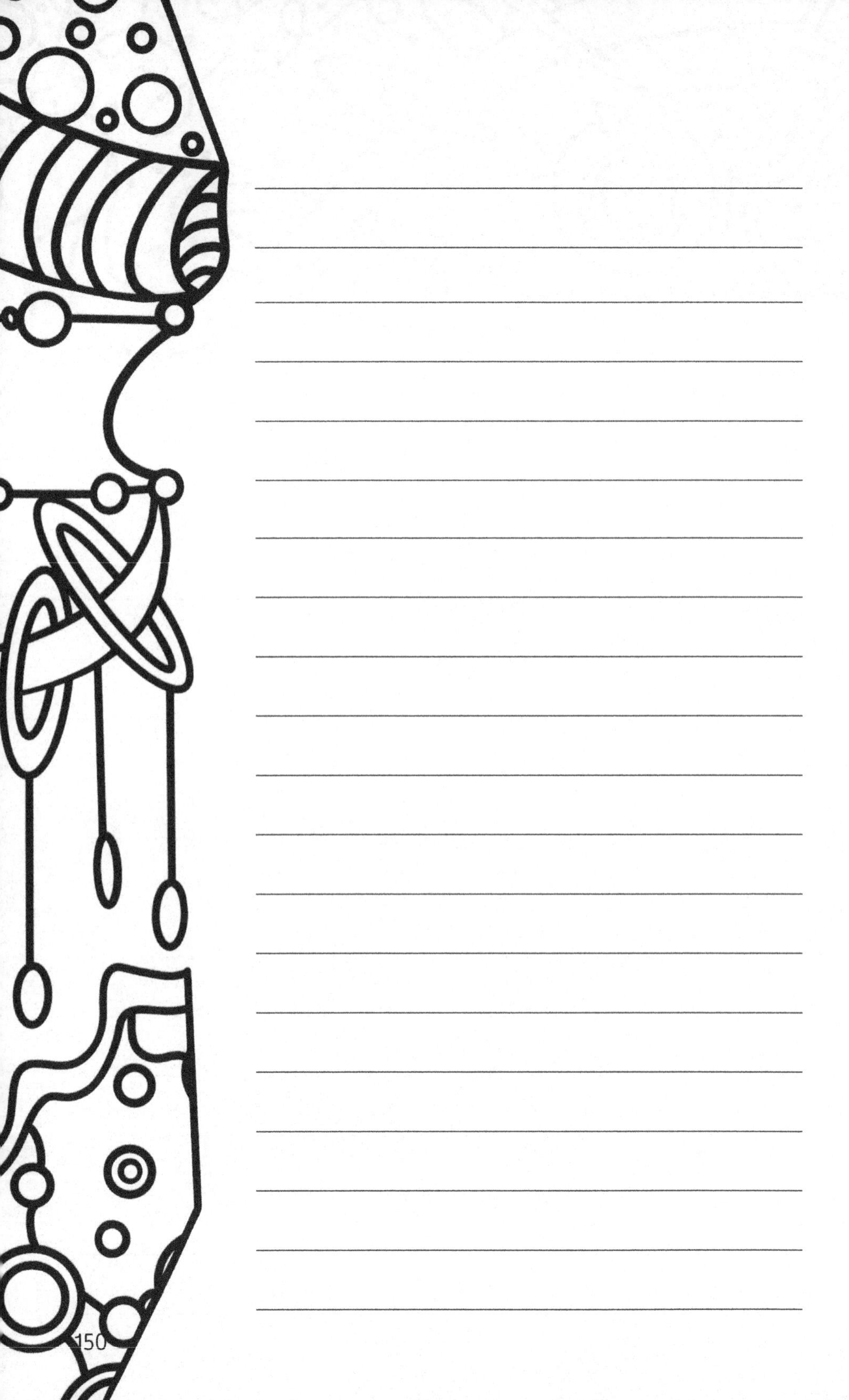

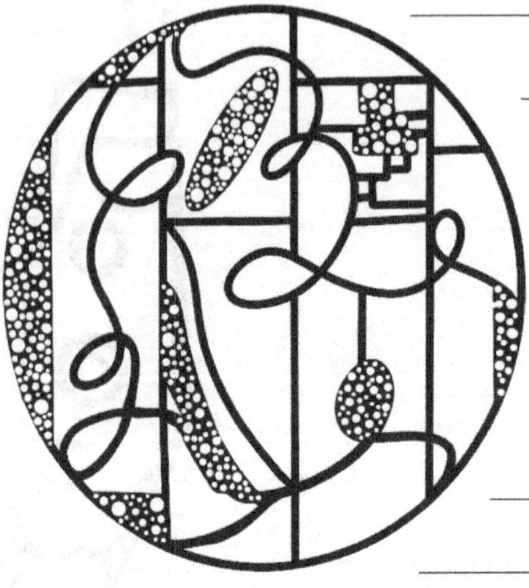

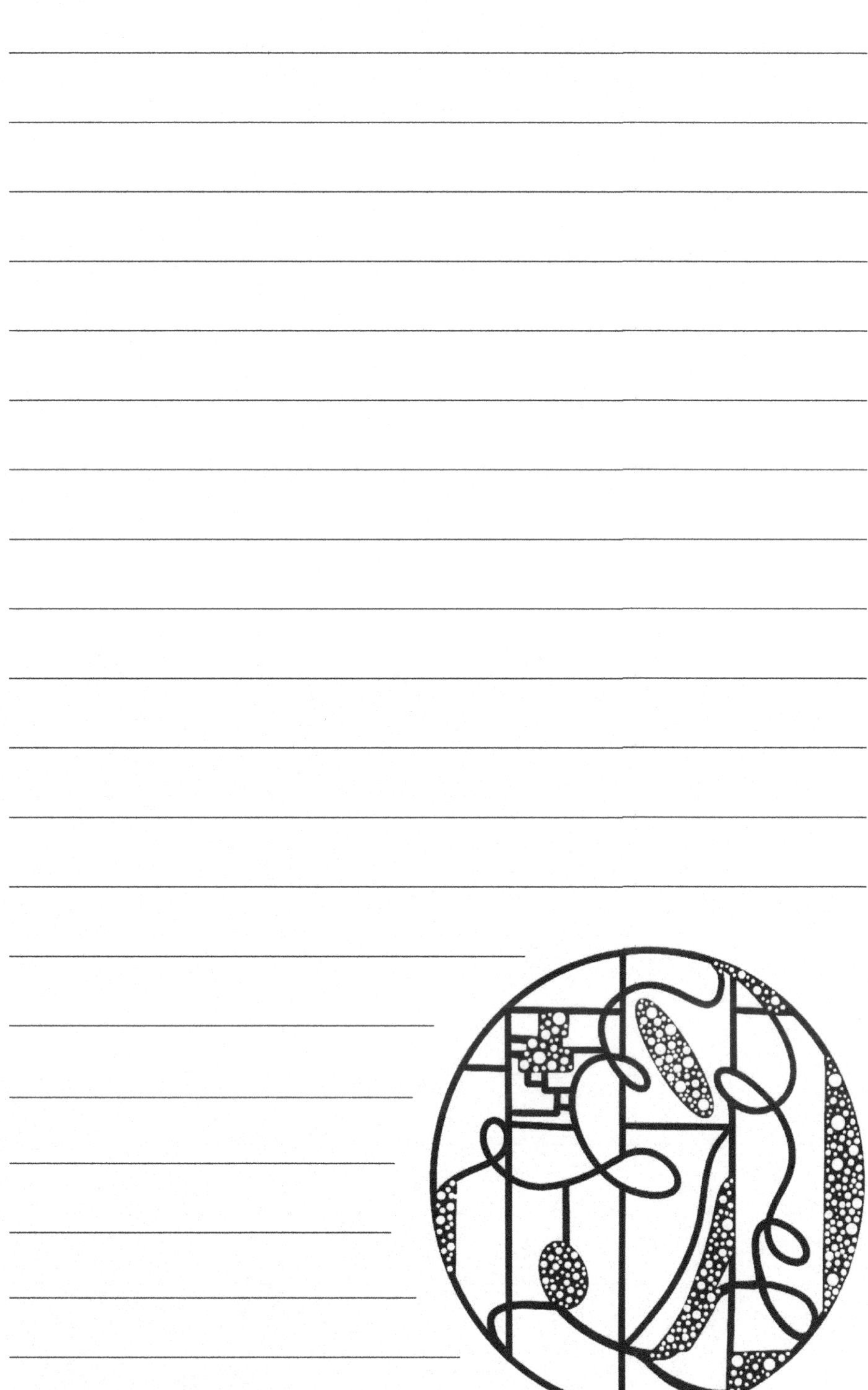

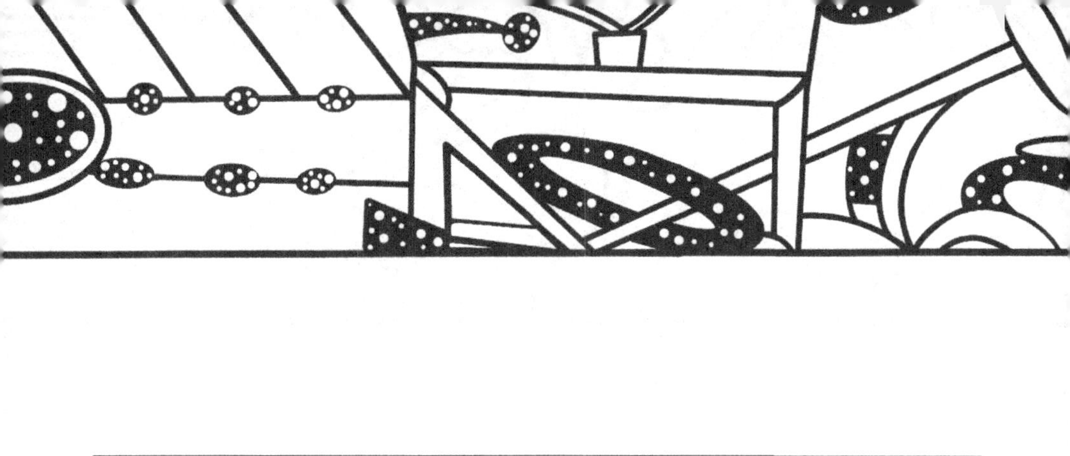

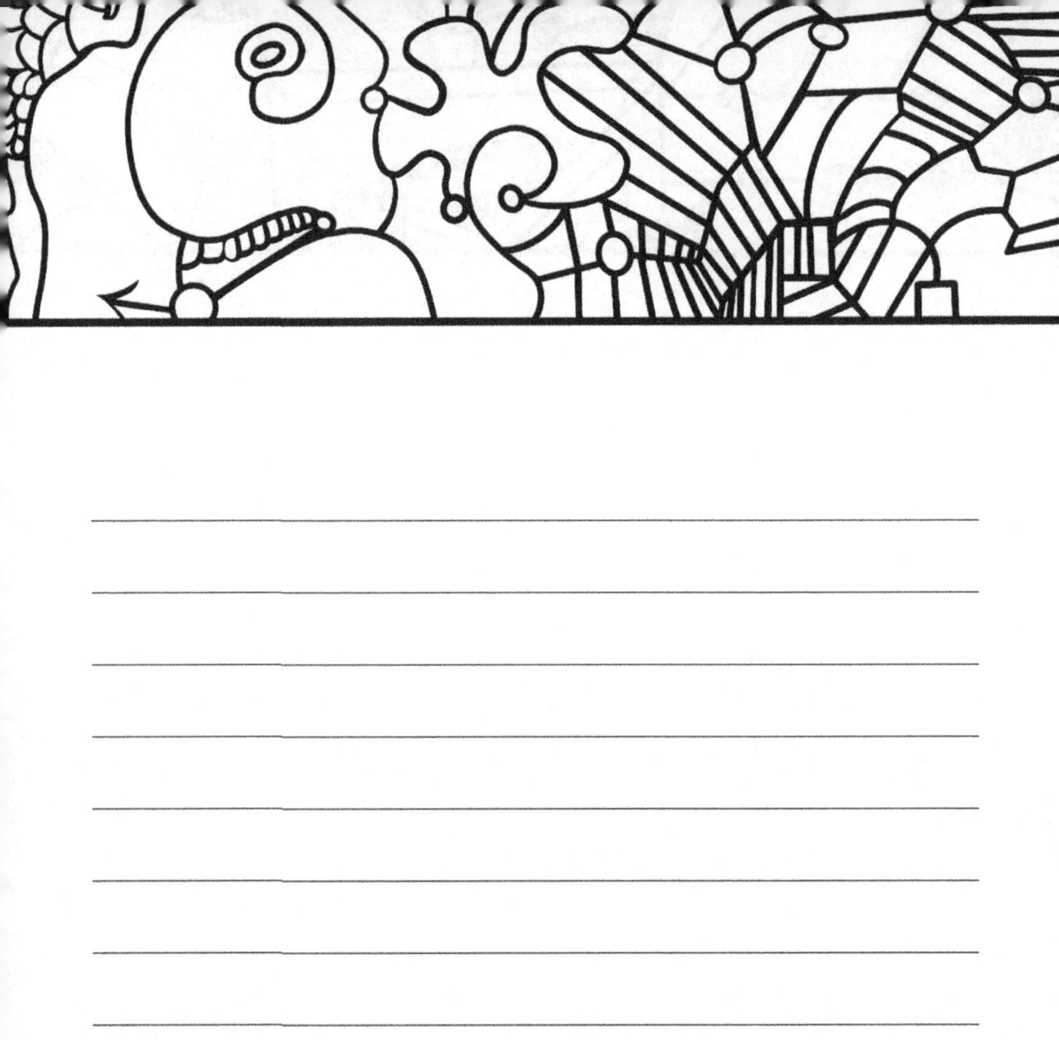

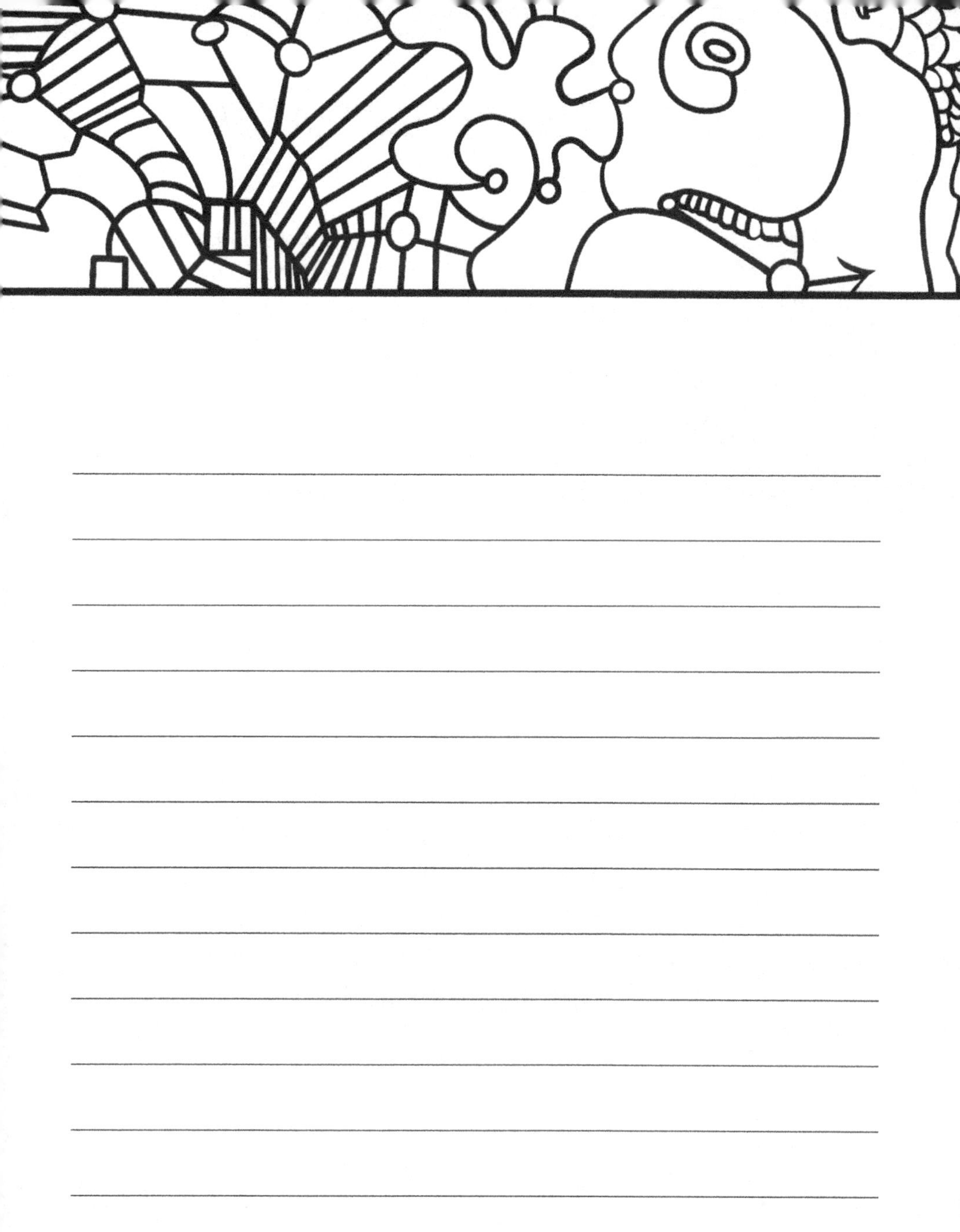

ABOUT THE ILLUSTRATOR

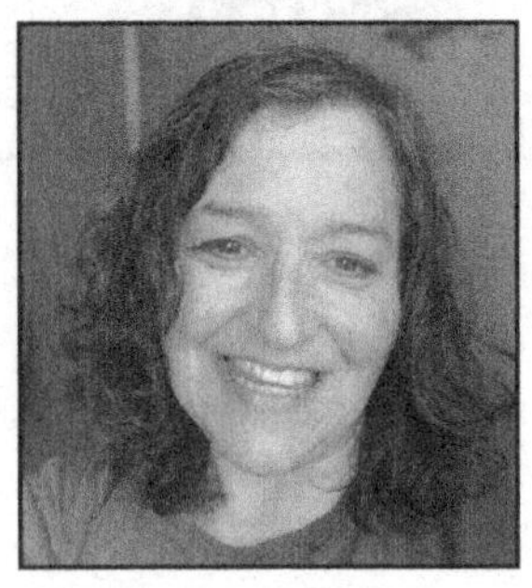

MICHELLE GAUTHIER has always had a passion for art in all its forms. As a child she would draw images in the dirt, on white mushrooms that lined the trees and in the frost that covered her Vermont farmhouse windows.

Her images are original and hand drawn. She pours time and love into the drawings and hopes that others enjoy coloring them as much as she enjoys drawing them. They can be colored upright or upside down, all one color in different hues, three colors or 100. It's up to you. There's no mistakes here. Just fun!

She invites you to join her on a creative adventure to discover your authentic selves!

If you enjoyed this journal please consider taking a moment to leave a review on Amazon.
Your input is invaluable, and sincerely appreciated!
—Michelle Gauthier

OTHER BOOKS BY MAKE NO MISTAKE COLORING

JOURNALS

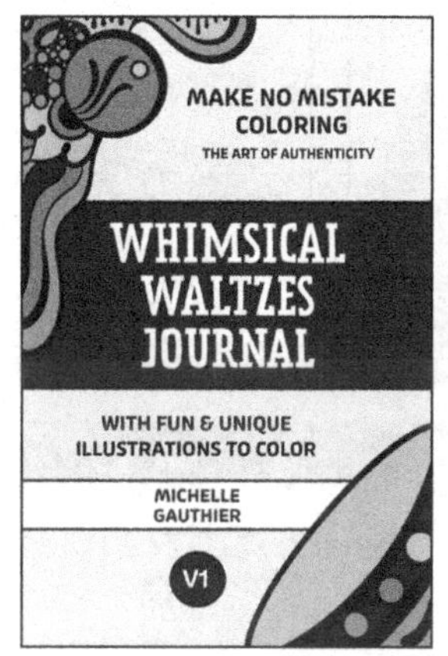

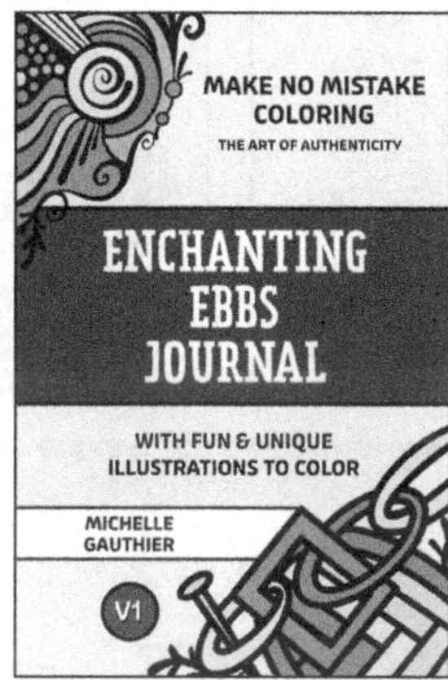

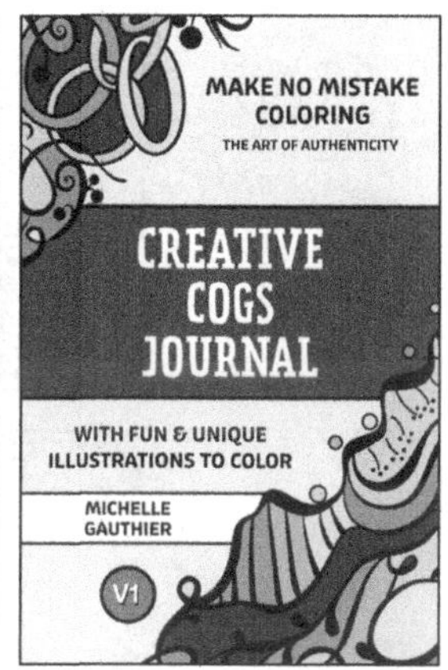

COLORING BOOKS

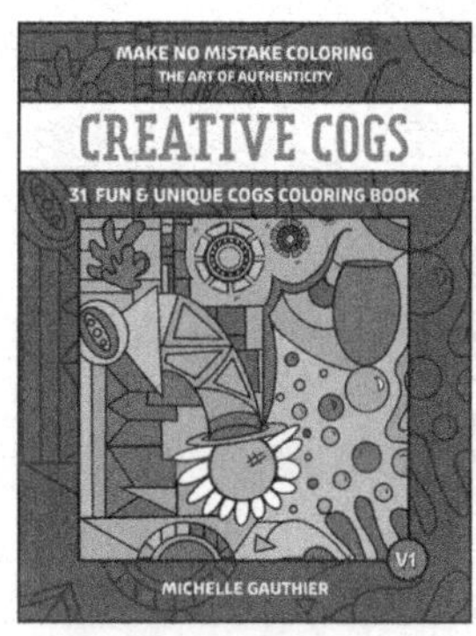

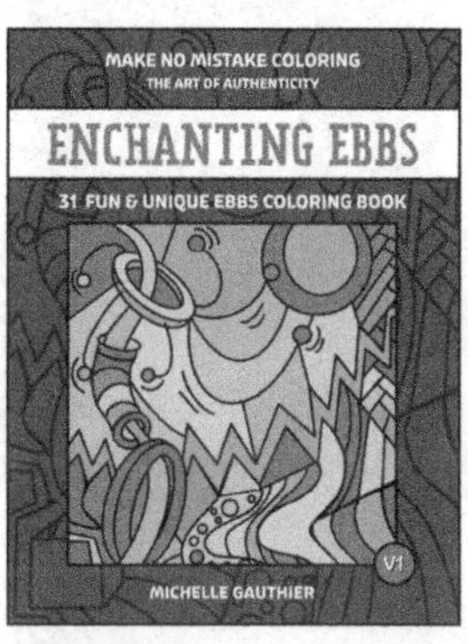

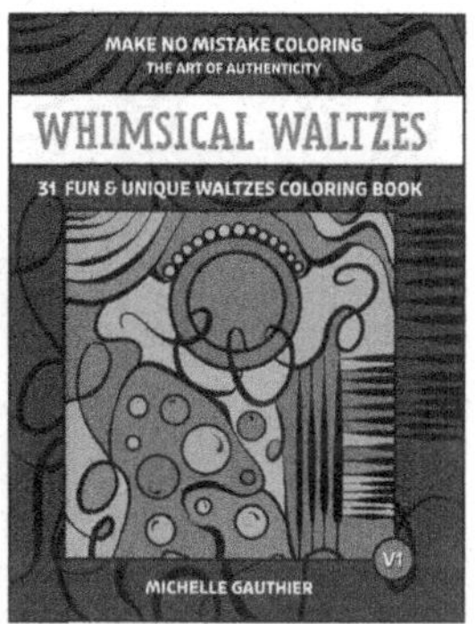

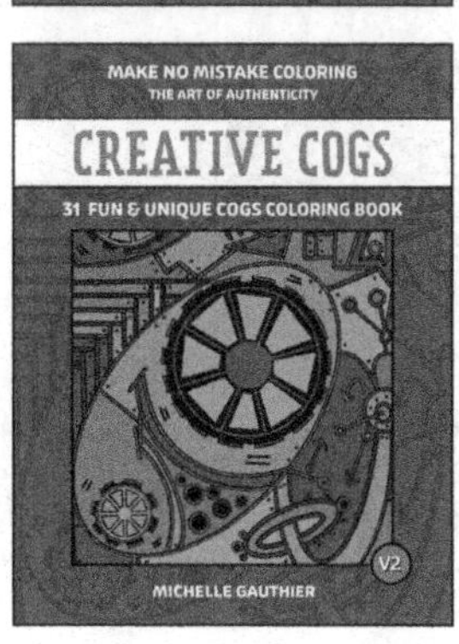

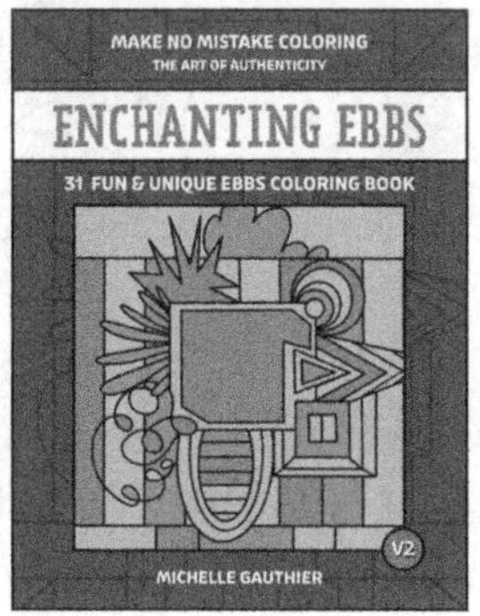

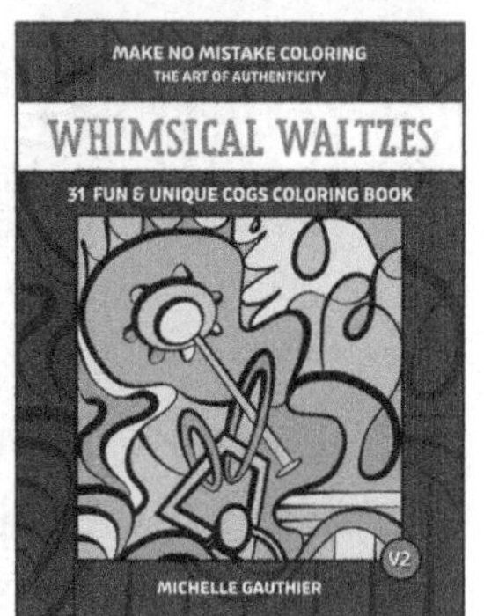

LOVE OUR ART?
CHECK OUT OUR OTHER PRODUCTS

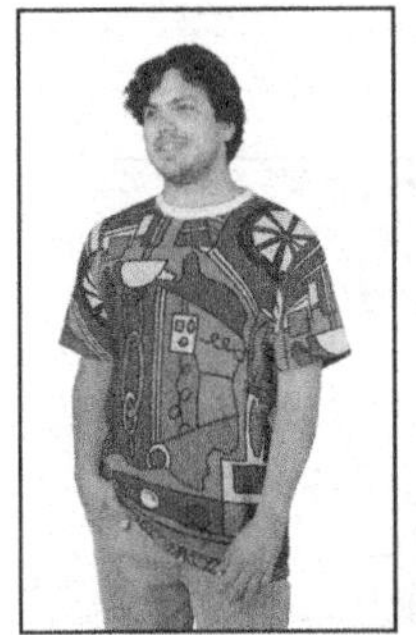
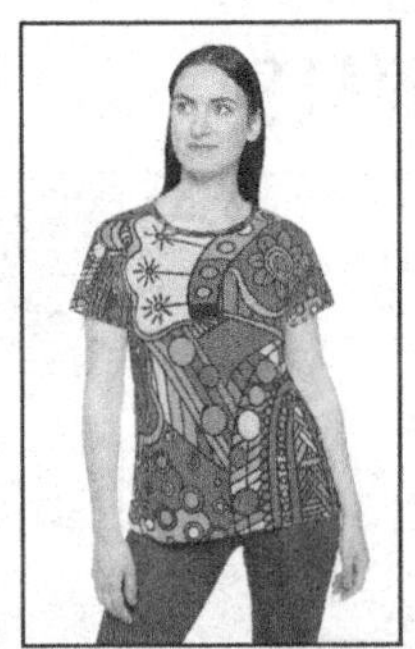
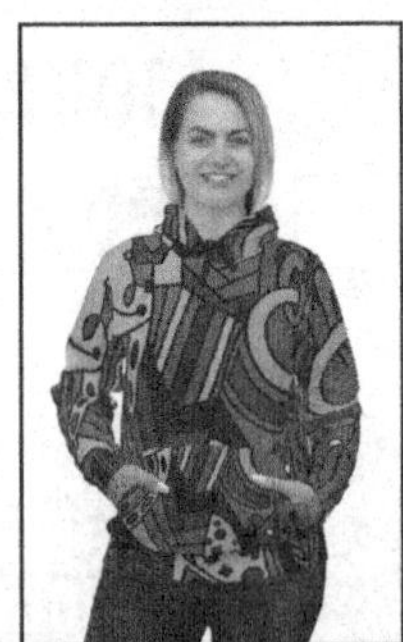
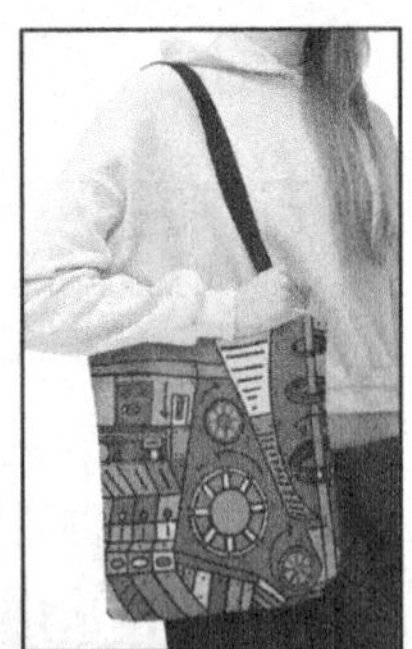
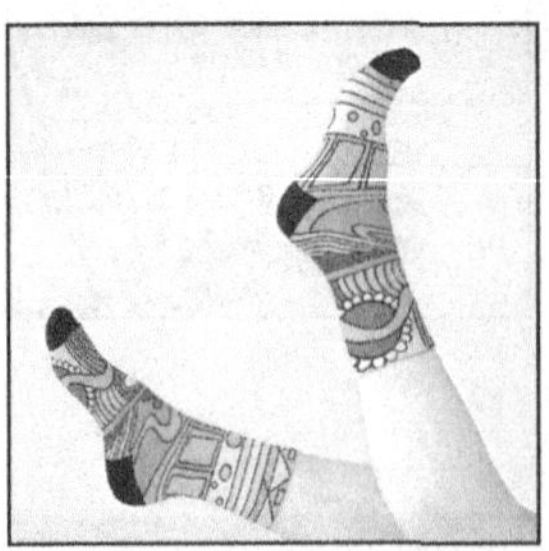
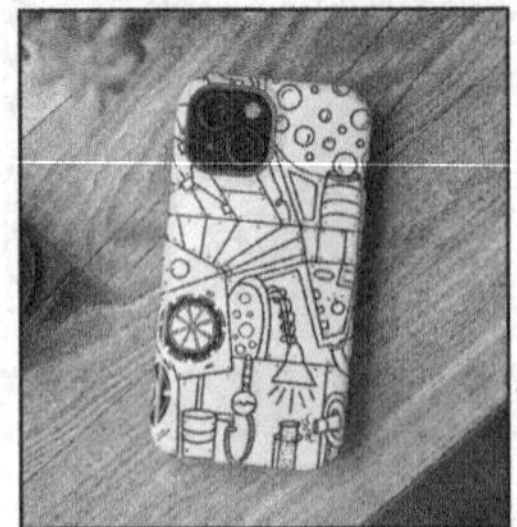
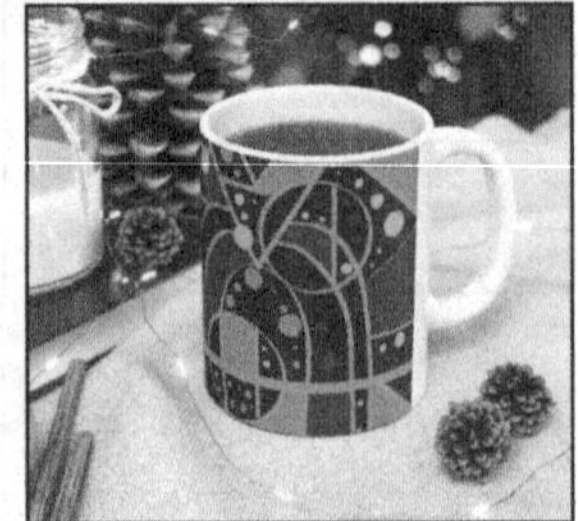
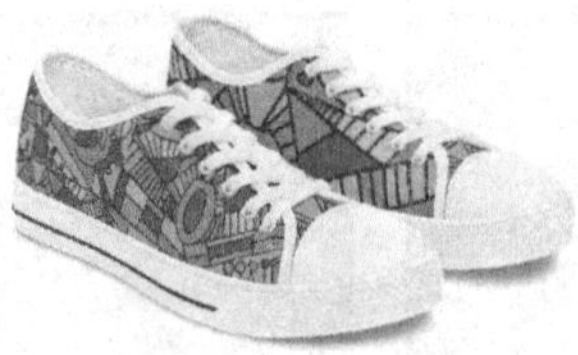
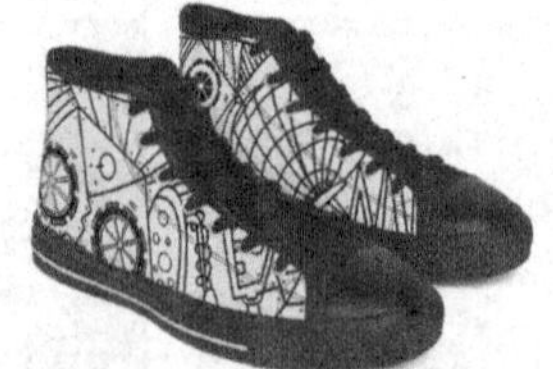

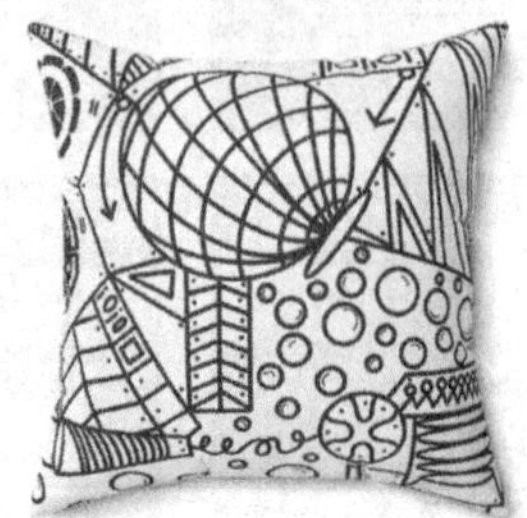

To learn more about Make No Mistake Coloring Products,
Visit our website at MakeNoMistakeColoring.com
or all titles are available on Amazon.com

Made in the USA
Coppell, TX
17 January 2026

68305742R10089